The Athenian Empire und
By J.L

THE ATHENIAN EMPIRE UNDER THE GUIDANCE OF PERICLES

Sect. 1. The Completion of the Athenian Democracy

To the Greeks of Cimon's day it might have seemed that the Athenian constitution as it had been fixed by Cleisthenes and further reformed after the battle of Marathon was as democratic as it well could be. But the supreme people was to become in still fuller measure lord in its own house, under the guidance of Ephialtes, whose career was suddenly cut short, and of Pericles, son of Xanthippus, who was to be the most prominent figure in Greece for thirty years. The mother of Pericles belonged to the family, and bore the name, of the daughter of the Sicyonian tyrant, the Agarista whose wooing had been so famous. She was the niece of Cleisthenes the lawgiver, and of Megacles who had been ostracized as a friend of the Pisistratids. The young statesman had a military training, but he came under the influence of two distinguished teachers, to whom he owed much. One was a countryman of his own, Damon of Oa, one of the most intellectual Athenians of his day, and renowned as a master of the theory of music. The other was an outlander and a philosopher, Anaxagoras of Clazomenae, whose mechanical theory of the material universe, once for all set in motion by an act of unchangeable mind, freed Pericles from the superstitions of the multitude whom it was his task to guide. To these masters the Statesman partly owed his intellectual aloofness; but he did not owe them either his political ideas or the gift of lucid and persuasive speech which was essential to his success. He was indeed a striking contrast to Cimon, the loose and genial boon companion. He seldom walked abroad; he was strict in the economy of his household; he avoided convivial parties; and jealously maintained the dignity of his reserve. His portrait was chiselled by Cresilas. It is something to have the round pedestal on which the original image was set, but we also possess a copy of the portrait. It shows us, not the lofty "Olympian" statesman, but the passionless contemplative face of the friend of Anaxagoras.

The most conservative institution in Athens was the Council of Areopagus, for it was filled up from the archons who were taken from the two richest classes in the state. This institution was incompatible with the development of democracy, and it was inevitable that it should be ended or mended. Ephialtes had prepared the way for an attack by accusing individual Areopagites of corruption and fraudulent practices; and then, taking advantage of Cimon's absence in Messenia, he introduced a series of laws which deprived the ancient council of all its powers that had any political significance. Its right to punish the public ministers and officers if they violated the laws, its duties of supervising the administration and seeing that the laws were obeyed, were taken away and transferred to the people. The censorial powers which enabled it to inquire into the lives of private citizens were abolished. Nothing was left to the venerable body but its jurisdiction in homicidal cases, the care of the sacred olive-trees of Athena, and a voice in the supervision of the property of the Eleusinian deities. The functions which it lost passed to the Council of Five Hundred, the Assembly, and the popular law-courts. All impeachments for crimes which threatened the public weal were henceforward brought before the Council or the Assembly; and henceforward the people tried in their own courts officials who had failed to give a satisfactory account of their administration.

We have a notable monument of the excitement which this radical change caused at Athens, in a drama of Aeschylus which was performed a few years later. The *Eumenides* describes the trial of Orestes on the hill of Ares for the murder of his mother, and the institution of the court of the Areopagus. The significance of the drama has been often misunderstood. It is no protest after the event; it is no cry to undo what had been done. On the contrary Aeschylus, so far as his poetical motive permits him to suggest a criticism of recent events, approves of the reform. The Areopagus, he suggests, was instituted as a court, not as a council; its true purpose is to pass a judgment on homicides, like Orestes. The *Eumenides* was calculated to tranquillise those who, awed by the dark and solemn associations which hovered over the hill of Ares, regarded the attack upon it as an impiety.

The dismantling of the Areopagus was an indirect blow to the dignity of the archons, who, by virtue of their office, became Areopagites. About the same time another step was • taken on the path of democracy by making the archonship a paid office. Once this was done, there was no longer any reason for confining the post to the two richer classes. The third class, the Zeugitae, were presently made eligible; and it cannot have been long before the Thetes, whose distinction from the third class seems to have been yearly becoming fainter, were admitted also.

The two engines of the democratic development were lot and pay. Lot had been long ago introduced; but it had not been introduced in its purest form. The archons and other lesser officers, and the members of the council, were taken by lot from a select number of candidates; but these candidates were chosen by deliberate election. This mixed system was now abolished; the preliminary election was done away with; and the Council of Five Hundred, as well as the archons, were appointed by lot from all the eligible citizens. By this means every citizen had an equal chance of holding political office, and taking a part in the conduct of public affairs.

It is clear that this system could not work unless the offices were paid; for the poor citizens would have been unable to give up their time to the service of the state. Accordingly pay was introduced not only for the archonship, but for the members of the Council. The payment of state offices was the leading feature of the democratic reforms of Pericles.

It was a feature which naturally won him popularity with the masses, especially when it was adopted in the case of the popular courts of justice. At the time of the attack on the Areopagus, Pericles carried a measure that the judges should receive a remuneration of an obol a day. Though the measure had the immediate political object of gaining popular support for the attack on the Areopagus, it was a measure which was ultimately inevitable. The amount of judicial business was growing so enormously that it would have been impossible to find a sufficient number of judges ready to attend day after day in the courts without any compensation. But the easily earned pay attracted the poor and idle, who found it pleasant to sit in court listening to curious cases, their sense of self-importance tickled by the flattering respect of the pleaders. Every citizen who wished could place his name on a list from which the list of judges was selected by lot, so many from each tribe; and the courts were empanelled from this list.

It was now to the interest of every Athenian that there should be as few citizens as possible to participate in the new privileges and citizenship, profits of citizenship. Accordingly, about ten years later the rolls the burghers were stringently revised; and a law was passed that the name of no child should be admitted whose father and mother were not Athenian citizens legitimately wedded. It was a law which would have excluded Themistocles and Cleisthenes the lawgiver, whose mothers were foreigners.

It was a matter of course that in cases of a political character the judges of the heliaea should be swayed by their own political opinions and by the eloquence of the pleaders working upon their emotions. It was inevitable that the legal aspect of such cases should be often lost to sight, and the facts often misjudged. It was an essential part of the democratic intention that the sovereign people should make its anger felt; and if its anger were sometimes, like a king's anger, unfair, that could not be helped. But it was far more serious that in private cases the ends of justice were liable to be defeated, not through intention but through ignorance. We can have no better evidence as to the working of the popular courts than the speeches by which the pleaders hoped to influence the decisions of the judges. Litigants at Athens had to plead their own cases; there was no such institution as court-advocates. But a man might learn off a speech which had been composed for him by another, and recite it in court. Hence there arose a class of professional speech-writers, and many of their speeches have been preserved. From these models of judicial eloquence we learn how pleaders expected to gain sentences in their favour. They make a large use of arguments which are perfectly irrelevant to the case; a plaintiff, for example, will try to demonstrate at great length that he has rendered services to the state and that his opponent has performed none. There was thus no question of simply administering the law. The judges heard each party interpreting the law in its own sense; but they had themselves no knowledge of the law, and therefore, however impartial they sought to be, their decision was unduly influenced by the dexterity of an eloquent pleader, and affected by considerations which had nothing to do with the matter at issue. And there was no appeal from their judgment.

A feature of the Athenian democracy, not to be lost sight of, is that public burdens were laid upon the rich burghers, which did not fall upon the poor. These were no regular taxes on income or capital, but burdens which were highly characteristic of ancient society, and which might fall to a man's lot only once or twice in his life. We have already seen how trierarchs were taken from the richer classes to equip and man triremes, in which they were themselves obliged to sail, and for which they were entirely responsible. It was a duty which entailed not only an outlay of money, but a considerable sacrifice of time and trouble. There were other burdens also. For example, when the city sent solemn deputations on some religious errand, whether to the yearly feast of Apollo at Delos, or to one of the great Panhellenic festivals, or to the oracle of Delphi, a wealthy citizen was chosen to eke out at his cost the money supplied for the purpose by the public treasury, and to conduct the deputation and equip it with magnificence worthy of the occasion. But none of the liturgies, as these public burdens were called, was more important or more characteristic of Athenian life than that of providing the choruses for the festivals of Dionysus. Every year each tribe named one of its wealthy tribesmen to be a *chorêgos*, and his duties were to furnish and array a chorus and provide a skilled trainer to teach it the dances and songs of the drama which it was to perform. Rivalry spurred the *chorêgoi* to ungrudging outlay. He whose chorus was victorious in the tragic or the comic competition was crowned and received a bronze tripod, which he used to set up, inscribed with his own name and that of his tribe, upon a pillar, or sometimes upon a miniature round temple. On the east side of the Acropolis, leading to the theatre, a long street of these choregic monuments recorded the public spirit of the citizens, and this Street of Tripods showed, perhaps more impressively than any other evidence, how much significance the state attached to the theatre and the worship of Dionysus. Never was piety more fully approved as wisdom. The state's endowment of religion turned out to be an endowment of brilliant genius; and the rich men who were called upon to spend their time and money in furnishing the dancers did service to the great masters of tragedy and comedy, and thereby served the whole world.

Sect. 2. War of Athens with the Peloponnesians

Alliance of The banishment of Cimon was the signal for a complete change in the foreign policy of Athens. She abandoned the alliance with the Lacedaemonians and formed a new alliance with their enemies, Argos and Thessaly. The new friendship of the Athenian and Argive peoples is reflected in the trilogy which Aeschylus composed about this time on the murder of Agamemnon and the vengeance of Orestes. The dramatist plays pointedly upon the alliance, and perhaps it is a not undesigned compliment to the new ally that he makes Agamemnon lord of Argos and not of newly-destroyed Mycenae. So far, indeed, as the main interests of Athens were concerned, she was not brought into direct collision with Sparta. But these interests forced her into deadly rivalry with two of Sparta's allies. The naval empire of Athens and the growth of her sea-power were rapidly extending her trade and opening new visions of commercial ambition in all quarters of the Greek world. She was competing with, and it seemed likely that she would outstrip, the two great cities of traffic, Corinth and Aegina. With Aegina there had already been a struggle, and now that Athens had grown in power and wealth another struggle was inevitable. The competition of Athenian merchants with Corinth in the west was active, and it was about this time that an Athenian general took Naupactus from the

Ozolian Locrians, and secured a naval station which gave Athens a considerable control over the mouth of the Corinthian Gulf. This was a blow which struck home; Athens had now the means of intercepting and harassing the Corinthian argosies which sailed forth with merchandise for the far west. War was a question of months, and the occasion soon came.

The Megarians, on account of a frontier dispute with Corinth, deserted the Peloponnesian league and placed themselves under Athenian projection. Nothing could be more welcome to Athens than the adhesion of Megara. Holding Megara, she had a strong frontier against the Peloponnesus, commanding the isthmus from Pagae on the Corinthian, to Nisaea on the Saronic, bay. Without any delays she set about the building of a double line of wall from the hill of Megara down to the haven of Nisaea, which faces Salamis, and she garrisoned these "Long Walls" with her own troops. Thus the eastern coast-road was under her control, and Attica had a strong of bulwark against invasion by land.

The occupation of Megara was a new offence to Corinth; and it was an offence to the mistress of the Peloponnesian league. War soon broke out, but at first Sparta took no active part. On the events of the war we are ill-instructed. We find an Athenian squadron making a descent on Halieis, and gaining an advantage over some Corinthian and Epidaurian troops. Then the little island of Cecryphalea, which lies between Aegina and the Argive shore, becomes the scene of a naval combat with a Peloponnesian fleet, and the Athenians prevail. At this point the Aeginetans enter the struggle. They saw that if Corinth sustained a severe defeat, their own fate was sealed; Athens would become absolute mistress in the Saronic sea. A great naval battle was fought near Aegina; the allies of both Aegina and Athens were engaged; and the Athenians, having taken seventy ships, landed on the island and blockaded the town. Thereupon the Peloponnesians sent a force of hoplites to help the Aeginetans; while the Corinthians, advancing over the heights of Geranea, descended into the Megarid, expecting that the

Athenians would find it impossible to protect Megara and blockade Aegina at the same time. But they reckoned without a true knowledge of the Athenian spirit. The citizens who were below and above the regular military age were formed into an extraordinary army and marched to the Megarid under the strategos Myronides. A battle was fought; both sides claimed the victory; but, when the Corinthians withdrew, the Athenians raised a trophy. Urged by the taunts of their fellow-citizens, the Corinthian soldiers returned in twelve days and began to set up a counter-trophy, but as they were at work the Athenians rushed forth from Megara and inflicted a severe defeat.

This warfare, round the shores and in the waters of the Saronic bay, is the prelude to more warfare in other parts of Greece; but it is a prelude which has a unity of its own. Athens is opposed indeed to the Peloponnesian alliance; but the war is, so far, mainly conducted by a concert of three states, whose interests lie in the neighbourhood of the Saronic Bay—Corinth, Epidaurus, and Aegina. These states have indeed the Peloponnesian league behind them, and are helped by "Peloponnesian ships" and "Peloponnesian hoplites"; but at the same time, the war has not yet assumed a fully Peloponnesian character.

The year of these successes was a year of intense excitement and strain for Athens; it might fairly be described as an *annus mirabilis* in her history. The victories of Cecryphalea and Aegina were won with only a portion of her fleet. For, in the very hour when she was about to be brought face to face with the armed opposition of rival Greek powers against the growth of her empire and the expansion of her trade, she had embarked in an enterprise beyond the limits of the Greek world. It was an expedition to Egypt, one of the most daring ventures she ever undertook.

A fleet of 200 Athenian and Confederate galleys was operating against Persia in Cyprian seas, when it was invited to cross over to Egypt. The call came from Inaros, a Libyan potentate, who had stirred up the lands of the lower Nile to revolt against their Persian masters. The murder of Xerxes had been followed by troubles at the Persian court, and it was some time before Artaxerxes was safely seated on his throne; the rebellion of Egypt was one of the consequences of this situation. The invitation of Inaros was most alluring. It meant that, if Athens delivered Egypt from Persian rule, she would secure the chief control of the foreign trade with the Nile valley and be able to establish a naval station on the coast; by one stroke she would far outstrip all the rival merchant cities of Hellas. The nameless generals of the Aegean fleet accepted the call of the Libyan prince. As in the days of remote antiquity, the "peoples of the north "were now to help the Libyans in an attempt to overthrow the lords of Egypt. Of those remote episodes the Greeks knew nothing, but they might remember how Carian and Ionian adventurers had once placed an Egyptian king upon the throne. In another way, an attack on Egypt was a step in a new path. Hitherto the Confederate ships had sailed in waters which were wholly or partly Greek, and had confined their purpose to the deliverance of Greek cities or cities which, like the Carian and Lycian, were in close touch with Greek civilisation. The shores of Cyprus, where Greek and Phoenician were side by side, invited above other shores a squadron of Greek deliverers. But when the squadron crossed over to Egypt, it entered a new sphere and undertook a new kind of work. The Egyptian expedition was an attempt to carry the struggle with Persia into another stage—a stage in which Greece is the aggressor and the invader. This attempt was not destined to prosper; more than a century was still to elapse before the invasion of Xerxes would be avenged. But it is well to remember that the Athenians, in moving on Egypt, anticipated Alexander the Great, and that success was not impossible if Cimon had been their general.

The Athenians sailed up the Nile to find Inaros triumphant, having gained a great victory in the Delta over a Persian army which had been sent to quell him. Sailing up they won possession of the city of Memphis, except the citadel, the "White Castle," in which the Persian garrison held out. After this achievement, we lose sight of the war in Egypt for more than two years, and beyond the protracted blockade of the White Castle we have no record how the Athenian forces were employed. But it was a fatal coincidence that the power of Athens should have been divided at this moment. With her full forces she might have inflicted a crushing blow on the Peloponnesians; with her full forces she might have prospered in Egypt. It was a triumph for the political party which had driven Cimon into banishment that, when half the Athenian fleet was on the banks of the Nile, the hostilities of Corinth and Aegina and their friends should have been so bravely repelled. Nothing impresses one more with the energy of Athens at this crisis than the stone which records the names of the citizens belonging to one of the tribes, who fell in this memorable year:

> Of the Erechtheid tribe,
> These are they who died in the war, in Cyprus, in Egypt, in
> Phoenice, at Halieis, in Aegina, at Megara, in the same year;

and the names follow.

The siege of Aegina was continued, and, within two years after the battle, the Aeginetans capitulated, and agreed to surrender their fleet and pay tribute to Athens. Few successes can have been more welcome or profitable to the Athenians than this. The island which offended their eyes and attracted their desires when they looked forth from their hill across the waters of their bay was at length powerless in their hands. They had lamed one of their most formidable commercial rivals; they had overthrown one of the most influential cities of Dorian Greece. In the Confederacy, Aegina took her rank with Thasos as the richest of the subject states. For these two island cities the burden of yearly tribute was thirty talents, incomparably larger than the sum paid by any of the other cities whose tribute we know.

In the meantime events in another part of Greece had led the Lacedaemonians themselves to take part in the war, and had transported the main interest of the struggle from the Saronic Gulf to Boeotia. The errand of the Lacedaemonians was an errand of piety, to succour their mother people, the Dorians of the north, one of whose three little towns had been taken by the Phocians. To force the aggressors to restore the place was an easy task for a force which consisted of 1500 Lacedaemonian hoplites and 10,000 troops of the allies. The real work of the expedition lay in Boeotia. It was clearly the policy of Sparta to raise up here a powerful state to hold Athens in check; and this could only be effected by strengthening Thebes and making her mistress of the Boeotian federation. Accordingly Sparta now set up the power of Thebes again, revising the league, and forcing the Boeotian cities to join it. When the army had done its work in Boeotia, its return to the Peloponnesus was beset by difficulties. To march through the Megarid was dangerous, for the Athenians held the passes, and had redoubled their precautions. And it was not safe to cross the Corinthian Gulf—the way by which they probably had come—for Athenian vessels were now on the watch to intercept them. In this embarrassment they seem to have resolved to march straight upon Athens, where the people were now engaged on the building of Long Walls from the city to the harbour. This course was probably suggested by an Athenian party of oligarchs, who were always abiding an opportunity to overthrow the democracy. The Peloponnesian army advanced to Tanagra, near the Attic frontier; but before they crossed the borders the Athenians went forth to meet them, 14,000 strong, including 1000 Argives and some Thessalian cavalry. The banished statesman, Cimon, now came to the Athenian camp, pitched on Boeotian soil, and sought leave to fight for his country—against Sparta. The request was hastily referred to the Council of Five Hundred at Athens; it was not granted; and all that Cimon could do was to exhort his partisans to fight valiantly. This act of Cimon prepared the way for his recall; in the battle which followed, his friends fought so stubbornly that none of them survived. There was great slaughter on both sides; but the Thessalian horsemen deserted during the combat, and the Lacedaemonians gained the victory. But the battle saved Athens, and the victory only enabled the victors to return by the Isthmus and cut down the fruit trees of the Megarid.

Athens now desired to make a truce with Sparta in order to gain time. No man was more fitted to compass this than the exile Cimon, whose recent conduct had shown that he was the foe of the foes of Athens, even if those foes were Spartans. The people, at the instance of Pericles, passed a decree recalling him; but when Cimon had negotiated the truce, he withdrew to a distance from Athens, with a tact which we might hardly have expected.

The Lacedaemonians celebrated their victory by a golden shield which they set above the gable of the new temple of Zeus in the altis of Olympia, as a gift from the spoils of Tanagra. But the victory did not even secure Boeotia. Two months after the battle, the Athenians made an expedition into Boeotia under the command of Myronides. A decisive battle was fought at Oenophyta, and the Athenians became masters of the whole land except Thebes. The Boeotian cities were not enrolled in the maritime Confederacy of Deles, but their dependence on Athens was expressed in the obligation of furnishing contingents to her armies. At the same time the Phocians entered into the alliance of Athens, and the Opuntian Locrians were constrained to acknowledge her supremacy. Such were the consequences of Oenophyta and Tanagra. Athens could now quietly complete the building of her Long Walls.

These brilliant successes were crowned, as we have seen, by the capture of Aegina; and probably about the same time the acquisition of Troezen gave the Athenians an important post on the Argolic shore. But in the far south their arms were not so prosperous. Since the capture of Memphis, no success seems to have been gained, and the White Castle still held out. After an ineffectual attempt to induce Sparta to cause a diversion by invading Attica, king Artaxerxes sent a large army to Egypt under Megabyzus, who was supported by a Phoenician fleet. Having won a battle, he drove the Greeks out of Memphis and shut them up in Prosopitis, an island formed by a canal which intersected the Canopic and Sebennytic channels of the Nile. Here he blockaded them for eighteen months. At last he drained the canal and turned aside the water, so that the Greek ships were left high and dry, and almost the whole island was reconnected with the banks. Thus the Persians were able to march across to the island. The Greeks having burned their ships retreated to Byblos, where they capitulated to Megabyzus and were allowed to depart. A tedious march brought them to friendly Cyrene, where they found means of returning to their homes. Inaros who kindled the revolt was crucified, though his life had been spared by the terms of the capitulation. Soon afterwards a relief squadron of fifty triremes arrived from Athens. It was attacked by the powerful Phoenician fleet in the Mendesian mouth of the Nile, and only a few ships escaped. The Persian authority was restored throughout the land; the day for Greek control of Egypt had not yet come.

But though the Athenians lost ships and treasure in this daring, ill-fated enterprise, their empire was now at the height of its power. They were even able to make the disaster in Egypt a pretext for converting the Delian confederacy into an undisguised Athenian empire. The triumphant Persian fleet might sail into the Aegean sea; Delos was not a safe treasury; the funds of the league must be removed to the Athenian Acropolis.

The empire of Athens now included a continental as well as a maritime dominion. The two countries which marched on her frontiers, Boeotia and Megara, had become her subjects. Beyond Boeotia, her dominion extended over Phocis and Locris to the pass of Thermopylae. In Argos her influence was predominant, Aegina had been added to her Aegean empire, the ships of Aegina to her navy. Through the subjection of Megara, the conquest of Aegina, and the capture of Troezen, the Saronic bay had almost been converted into an Attic lake.

The great commercial city of the isthmus was the chief and most dangerous enemy of Athens, and the next object of the policy of Pericles was to convert the Corinthian Gulf into an Attic lake also, and so hem in Corinth on both her seas. The possession of the Megarid and Boeotia, and especially the station at Naupactus, gave Athens control of the northern shores of the gulf, from within the gate up to the isthmus. But the southern seaboard was still entirely Peloponnesian; and outside the gate, on the Acarnanian coast, there were posts which ought to be secured. The general Tolmides made a beginning by capturing the Corinthian colony Chalcis, opposite Patrae. Then Pericles himself conducted an expedition to continue the work of Tolmides. Having failed to reduce Sicyon he laid siege to Oeniadae, an important and strong-walled mart on the Acarnanian coast, but was unable to take it. Though no military success was gained, the expedition created a sensation, and it seems to have led to the adhesion of the Achaean cities to the Athenian alliance. It is certain at least that shortly afterwards Achaea was an Athenian dependency; and for a few years Athenian vessels could sail with a sense of dominion in the Corinthian as well as in the Saronic bay.

Sect. 3. Conclusion of Peace with Persia

The warfare of recent years had been an enormous strain on the resources of Athens, and it was found necessary to increase the burden of tribute imposed on her allies. She wanted a relief from the strain, but after the expedition of Pericles three or four years elapsed before peace was concluded. During that interval there seems to have been by mutual consent of the combatants a cessation from military operations. Lacedaemon and Argos first concluded a treaty of peace for thirty years; and then Cimon, who had returned to Athens, negotiated a truce, which was fixed for five years, between the Athenians and Peloponnesians.

As soon as the peace was arranged, Athens and her allies were able to resume their warfare against Persia, and to no man could that warfare be more safely or fitly entrusted than to the hero of the Eurymedon river. Pericles may have been well pleased to use Cimon's military experience; and an amicable arrangement seems to have been made, Cimon undertaking not to interfere with the policy of Pericles. Gossip said that Cimon's sister had much to do with bringing to pass the reconciliation. "The charms as well as the intrigues of Elpinice appear to have figured conspicuously in the memoirs of Athenian biographers: they were employed by one party as a means of calumniating Cimon, by the other for discrediting Pericles." But we need not heed the gossip. Women played no part in the history of Athena's city.

The Phoenician fleet, which had put down the Egyptian rebellion, was afterwards sent to re-establish the authority of Artaxerxes in the island of Cyprus; and accordingly Cimon sailed thither with a squadron of 200 vessels. He detached sixty to help a princelet who had succeeded in defying the Persians in the fens of the Delta of the Nile; for the Athenians, even after their calamity, had not entirely abandoned the thought of Egyptian conquest. Then he laid siege to Cition. It was the last enterprise of the man who had conducted the war against Persia ever since the battle of Mycale. He died during the blockade; and his death marks the beginning of a new period m which hostilities between Greek and Persian slumber. But one final success was gained. Raising the siege of Cition, because there was no food, the fleet arrived off Salamis, and the Greeks gained a double victory by sea and land over the Phoenician and Cilician ships.

But this victory did not encourage the Athenians to continue the war. We have no glimpse of the counsels of their statesmen at this moment; but the facts of the situation enable us to understand their resolution to make peace with the Great King. The events of recent years had proved to them that it was beyond the strength of Athens to carry on war at the same time, in any effectual way, with the common enemy of all the Greeks and with her rivals among the Greeks themselves. It was therefore necessary to choose between peace with Persia and peace in Greece. But an enduring peace in Greece could only be purchased by the surrender of those successes which Athens had lately gained. Corinth would never acquiesce, until she had won back her old predominant position in her western gulf; so long as she was hemmed in, as Athens had hemmed her in, she would inevitably seize any favourable hour to strike for her release. Some Athenian politicians would have been ready to retreat from the positions which had been recently seized and of which the occupation was most galling to Corinth. But Pericles, who had won those positions, was a strong imperialist. The aim of his statesmanship was to increase the Athenian empire and to spread the political influence of Athens within the borders of Greece. He was unwilling to let any part of her empire go, for the sake of earning new successes against the barbarian. The death of Cimon, who had been the soul of the Persian war, may have helped Pericles to carry through his determination to bring that war to an end. And the Great King on his side was disposed to negotiate; for the Greek victory of Cyprian Salamis had been followed by a revolt of Megabyzus, the general who had quelled the insurrection of Egypt.

Accordingly peace was made with Persia. There is a dark mist about the negotiations, so dark that it has been questioned whether a formal treaty was ever concluded. But there can be no reasonable doubt that Athens came to an understanding with Artaxerxes, and that peace ensued; and it is equally certain that there was a definite contract, by which Persia undertook not to send ships of war into the Aegean, and Athens gave a similar pledge securing the coasts of the Persian empire against attack. An embassy from Athens and her allies must have waited on the Great King at Susa; and the terms of the arrangement must have been put in writing. But, on the other hand, there was no treaty as between two Greek states. The Great King would never have consented to treat either with a Greek city or a federation of Greek cities as an equal. And he certainly did not stoop to the humiliation of formally acknowledging the independence of the Greek cities of Asia. It was enough that he should graciously promise to make certain concessions. But, whatever were the diplomatic forms of the agreement, both parties meant peace, and peace was maintained. It has been called the Peace of Callias; and we have a record which makes it probable that the chief ambassador was Callias, the richest man at Athens, and the husband of Cimon's sister.

The first act in the strife of Greece and Persia thus closes. All the cities of Hellas which had come under barbarian sway had been reunited to the world of free Hellenic states; except in one outlying corner. The Greek cities of Cyprus were left to struggle with the

Phoenicians as best they might; and the Phoenicians soon got the upper hand and held it for many years. They tried to extirpate Greek civilisation from the island; but Greek civilisation was a hardy growth, and we shall hereafter see Greek dynasties again in power.

Sect. 4. Athenian Reverses. The Thirty Years' Peace

The peace with Persia, however, was not followed by further Athenian expansion within the defined limits; on the contrary, some of the most recent acquisitions of the Athenian empire began to fall away. Orchomenus and Chaeronea and some other towns in western Boeotia were seized by exiled oligarchs; and it was necessary for Athens to intervene promptly. The general Tolmides went forth with a wholly inadequate number of troops. He took and garrisoned Chaeronea, but did not attempt Orchomenus. On his way home he was set upon by the exiles from Orchomenus and some others, in the neighbourhood of Coronea, and defeated. He was himself slain; many of the hoplites were taken prisoners; and the Athenians in order to obtain their release resigned Boeotia. Thus the battle of Coronea undid the work of Oenophyta.

Athens had little reason to regret this loss; for dominion in Boeotia was not really conducive to the consolidation of her empire. To maintain control over the numerous city-states of the Boeotian country would have been a constant strain on her military resources, which would hardly have been remunerative. The loss of Boeotia was followed by the loss of Phocis and Locris. It was strange enough that Phocis should fall away. A few years before the Phocians had taken possession of Delphi. The Spartans had sent an army to rescue the shrine from their hands, and give it back to the Delphians; but as soon as the Spartans had gone, an Athenian army came, led by Pericles, and restored the sanctuary to the Phocians. It was a Sacred War, but so conducted that it did not make a breach of the Five Years' Truce. Yet, although their position at Delphi seemed to depend on the support of Athens, the Phocians now deserted her alliance. The change was due to an oligarchical reaction in the Phocian cities, consequent on the oligarchical rising in Boeotia.

The defeat of Coronea dimmed the prestige of Athenian arms; and still more serious results ensued. Euboea and Megara revolted at the same moment; here too oligarchical parties were at work. Pericles, who was a general, immediately went to Euboea with the regiments of seven of the tribes, while those of the remaining three marched into the Megarid. But he had no sooner reached the island than he was overtaken by the news that the garrison in the city of Megara had been massacred and that a Peloponnesian army was threatening Attica. He promptly returned, and his first object was to unite his forces with the troops in the Megarid, which were under the command of Andocides. But king Pleistoanax and the Lacedaemonians were, between them, commanding the east coast-road. Andocides was compelled to return to Attica by creeping round the corner of the Corinthian Gulf at Aegosthenae and passing through Boeotia. The troops were guided by a man of Megara named Pythion, and the gratitude of the three tribes "whom he saved by leading them from Pagae, through Boeotia, to Athens" was recorded on his funeral monument. The stone has survived, and the verses written upon it are a touching reminiscence of a moment of great peril. But when the whole army united in Attica, the peril was passed. The return of Pericles had disconcerted king Pleistoanax, who commanded the Lacedaemonians, and having advanced only as far as the Thriasian plain he withdrew, deeming it useless to strike at Athens. Pericles was thus set free to carry out the reduction of Euboea. Histiaea, the city in the north of the island, was most hardly dealt with, probably because her resistance was most obstinate; the people were driven out, their territory annexed to Athens; and the new settlement of Oreos took the place of Histiaea. In other cases the position of each state was settled by an agreement; and the arrangements which were made with Chalcis are still preserved on stone. The alarm of the Athenians is reflected in reductions of tribute which they allowed to their subject states; they feared that the example of Euboea might spread. The truce of five years was now approaching its end, and peace was felt to be so indispensable that they resigned themselves to purchasing a more durable treaty by considerable concessions. They had lost Megara, but they still held the two ports, Nisaea and Pagae. These, as well as Achaea, they agreed to surrender, and on this basis a peace was concluded for thirty years between the Athenians and the Peloponnesians. All the allies of both sides were enumerated in the treaty, and it was stipulated that neither Athens nor Lacedaemon was to admit into her alliance an ally of the other, while neutral states might join whichever alliance they chose.

It was a humiliating peace for Athens, and perhaps would not have been concluded but for the alarm which had been caused by the inroad of the Peloponnesians into Attic territory. While the loss of Boeotia was probably a gain, and the evacuation of Achaea might be lightly endured, the loss of the Megarid was a serious blow. For, while Athens held the long walls and the passes of Geranea, she had complete immunity from Peloponnesian invasions of her soil. Henceforth Attica was always exposed to such aggressions. Besides this, her position in the Crisaean Gulf was greatly weakened. The attempt which she had made to win a land-empire had succeeded only for a brief space; the lesson was that she must devote her whole energy to maintaining her maritime dominion. It was a gloomy moment for the Athenians; and it must have required all the tact and eloquence of Pericles to restore the shaken confidence and revive the drooping spirits. Euboea at all events was safe, and men might look back over sixty years to that victory which had been won by their ancestors, in a critical hour, over a joint attack of the Boeotians and Chalcidians. On that occasion a tithe of the spoil had been dedicated to Athena. Pericles now set up a bronze chariot with this tithe, and so associated the earlier victory with his own. The parallel was close; for the rebellion of Euboea had been mainly instigated by the Boeotian oligarchs who freed their own land from Athenian control. The marble base on which the chariot stood, on the Acropolis, has been found, and a few letters of the inscribed verses, which Herodotus read and copied, can be made out. The recollection that the sons of the Athenians "quenched the insolence" of the Boeotians, as those verses have it, was indeed the only consolation that could be offered for the defeat of Coronea. While he made the most of the reduction of Euboea, Pericles may have also dwelt on the prospects of the Attic sea-empire. He may have elated them by words such as he is reported to have used at a later moment of despondency. "Of the two divisions of the world accessible to man, the land and the sea, there is one of which you are absolute masters, and have, or may have, the dominion to any extent you please. Neither the Great King nor any nation on earth can hinder a navy like yours from penetrating whithersoever you choose to sail."

Sect. 5. The Imperialism of Pericles, and the Opposition to his Policy

The cities of the Athenian alliance might have claimed, when the Persian war was ended, that the "Confederacy" should be broken up and that they should resume their original and rightful freedom. The fair answer to this claim would have been, that peace had indeed come, but that it would endure only so long as a power was maintained strong enough to stand up against the might of Persia, Dissolve the Confederacy, and the cities will severally and speedily become the prey of the barbarian. But in any case, the Confederacy had become an Empire, and Athens was in the full career of an ambitious "imperialist" state. The tributes which she imposed on her subjects were probably not oppressive, and were constantly revised; when the Five Years' Truce was about to be concluded, she reduced the tribute, which had been increased under the stress of the war, to its former amount. She did not force her own coinage upon her subjects; every city might have its own mint, and most of them had. But there was much that was galling in her empire, to communities in which the love of freedom was strongly developed. The revolt and reduction of Euboea showed in its undisguised shape the rule of might. It must however be remembered, in judging of the feelings of the cities towards their mistress, that in nearly every city there were an oligarchical and a democratical party. The democracy was supported by Athens and was generally friendly to her; the oligarchs were always on the watch for an opportunity to rebel. And for this reason, a revolt is not in itself evidence that Athens was unpopular among her allies. The Carian and Lycian cities began to fall away after the peace with Persia; ^ but most of them were only superficially Hellenized, and Athens let them go, not thinking it worth while to take measures for retaining her control of them.

Pericles had been the guide of the Athenian people in the recent war; his counsels had directed their imperial policy. But that policy had not been unchallenged; his leadership had not been unopposed.

There was a strong oligarchical party at Athens which not only disliked the democracy of their city, but arraigned her empire. Most of this party attacked the imperialist policy of Pericles purely from party motives, and for the purpose of attacking him; but there was one man at least who may claim Ihe credit of having honestly espoused the cause of the allied cities against the unscrupulous selfishness of his own city. This was Thucydides, the son of Melesias, a man who had connexions with many of the allies. He maintained that the tribute should be reserved exclusively for the purpose for which it was levied, the defence of Greece against Persia, and that Athens had no right to spend it on other things, especially on things which concerned herself alone, and did not benefit the cities. It was an injustice that these cities should have to defray any part of the costs of an Athenian campaign in Boeotia or of a new temple in Athens. This was a just view, but justice is never entirely compatible with the growth of a country to political greatness, and Pericles was resolved to make his country great at all hazards. For this purpose his policy towards the allied cities was—in a phrase which seems to have been his own—"to keep them well in hand." It is pleasant to find that voices were raised against his unscrupulous imperialism.

The more extreme section of the party which supported Thucydides would not have hesitated to betray Athens into the hands of her foes for the sake of overthrowing the democracy. They had tried to do this at the time of the battle of Tanagra. Much less would they have scrupled to give secret help to the oligarchical parties which worked against Athenian rule in the subject cities. Oligarchy had raised its head in many places during the Five Years' Truce. Oligarchical movements had led to the loss of Boeotia; oligarchical movements had caused the revolts of Megara and Euboea; oligarchy had even prevailed in Phocis. There can be little doubt that this widespread oligarchical activity had its echo in Athens; and that in these years the party opposed to Pericles was loud and aggressive. He met that opposition with remarkable dexterity. He introduced a new policy, which, while it was thoroughly imperialist, was so popular at Athens that his adversaries were silenced.

Among the measures which Pericles initiated to strengthen the empire of his city, none was more important in its results than the system of settling Athenian citizens abroad. Like measures of many great statesmen, this policy effected the solution of two diverse problems. The colonies which were thus sent to different parts of the empire, served as garrisons in the lands of subject allies, and they also helped to provide for part of the superfluous population of Athens. The first of these Periclean *cleruchies* was established in the Thracian Chersonese, under the personal supervision of Pericles himself. Lands were bought from the allied cities of the peninsula, and a thousand Athenian citizens, chiefly of the poor and unemployed, were allotted farms and assigned to the several cities. The payment for the land was made in the shape of a reduction of the tribute. At the same time Pericles restored the wall which Miltiades had built across the isthmus, to protect the country against the Thracians; in view of the rising power of the Thracian prince Teres, this precaution was wise.

The out-settlements in the Chersonese—which were probably followed by out-settlements in Lemnos and Imbros, the island warders of the gate of the Propontis—were the most important of all. The same policy was at the same time adopted in Euboea and some of the islands of the Aegean, and in a mysterious place, the Thracian Brea, which probably lay west of the Strymon. The original act of the colonisation of Brea has been preserved, and the provision that all the settlers shall belong to the two poorest classes of the people, on the Solonian classification, illustrates the character of the Periclean cleruchies. The policy was naturally popular at Athens, since it provided for thousands of unemployed who cumbered the streets; and perhaps it may be regarded as one of the happiest strokes devised by Pericles for increasing his ascendency and confounding his opponents. But it was a policy which was highly unpopular among the allies, in whose territories the settlements were made; and it gave perhaps more dissatisfaction than any other feature of Athenian rule.

Most Athenian citizens were naturally allured by a policy of expansion which made their city great and powerful without exacting heavy sacrifices from themselves. The day had not yet come when they were unwilling to undertake military service, and they were content as long as the cost of maintaining the empire did not tax their purses. The empire furthered the extension of their trade, and increased their prosperity. The average Athenian burgher was not hindered by his own full measure of freedom from being willing to press, with as little scruple as any tyrant, the yoke of his city upon the necks of other communities. So long as the profits of empire were many and its burdens light, the Athenian democracy would feel few searchings of heart in adopting the imperialism of Pericles.

That imperialism was indeed of a lofty kind. The aim of the statesman who guided the destinies of Athens in these days of her greatness was to make her the queen of Hellas; to spread her sway on the mainland as well as beyond the seas; and to make her political influence felt in those states which it would have been unwise and perhaps impossible to draw within the borders of her empire. The full achievement of this ideal would have meant the union of all the Greeks, an union held together by the power of Athens, but having a natural support in a common religion, common traditions, common customs, and a common language.

Shortly before the loss of Boeotia through the defeat of Coronea, Athens addressed to Greece an open declaration of her Panhellenic ambition. She invited the Greek states to send representatives to an Hellenic congress at Athens, for the purpose of discussing certain matters of common interest. To restore the temples which had been burned by the Persians, to pay the votive offerings which were due to the gods for the great deliverance, and to take common measures for clearing the seas of piracy;—this was the programme which Athens proposed to the consideration of Greece. The invitation did not go to the west, for the Italiots and Siceliots were not directly concerned in the Persian war, but it went to all the cities of old Greece, and to the cities and islands which belonged to the Athenian empire. If the congress had taken place it would have inaugurated an amphictiony of all Hellas, and Athens would have been the centre of this vast religious union. It was a sublime project, but it could not be. It was not to be expected that Sparta would fall in with a project which, however noble and pious it sounded, might tempt or help Athens to strike out new and perilous paths of ambition and aggrandisement. The Athenian envoys were rebuffed in the Peloponnesus, and the plan fell through. Immediately after this, the revolution in Boeotia deprived Athens of her empire on the mainland.

Sect. 6. The Restoration of the Temples

It remained then for Athens to carry out that part of the programme which concerned herself, and restore in greater splendour the temples of her city and her land. We shall miss the meaning of the architectural monuments which now began to rise under the direction and influence of Pericles, if we do not clearly grasp their historical motive, and recognise their immediate connexion with the Persian war. It devolved upon the city, as a religious duty, to make good the injuries which the barbarian had inflicted upon the habitations of her gods, and fully to pay her debt of gratitude to heaven for the defeat of the Mede. And seeing that Athens had won her great empire through that defeat, the gods might well expect that she would perform this duty on no small scale and in no niggardly spirit. In this, above all, was the greatness of Pericles displayed, that he discerned the importance of performing them on a grand scale. He recognised that the city by ennobling the houses of her gods would ennoble herself; and that she could express her own might and her ideals in no worthier way than by the erection of beautiful temples. His architectural plans went farther than this, and we can see that he was influenced by the example of the Pisistratids; but the chief buildings of the Periclean age, it should always be remembered, were, like the Athenian empire itself, the direct consequence of the Persian invasion.

Of the monuments which in the course of twenty years changed the appearance of the Acropolis, one of the first was a gigantic statue of Athena, wrought in bronze. The goddess stood near the west brow of her own hill, looking south-westward, and her helmet and the tip of her lance flashing in the sun could be seen far off at sea. But nothing was so pressing as to carry to completion the new house of the goddess, which had been begun in the days of Themistocles and never finished. The work was now resumed on the same site, and the same foundations; but it was resumed on an entirely different plan, which was drawn up by the gifted architect Ictinus. The new temple was slightly broader but considerably shorter than it would have been if the old design had been carried out, and instead of foreign Parian marble, native Attic from the quarries of Pentelicus was employed. Callicrates, another expert architect, superintended the execution of the plan which Ictinus had conceived. It is not within our province to enter here into the architectural beauties of this perfect Dorian temple, which came afterwards to be generally known as the Parthenon. The building contained two rooms, between which there was no communication. The eastern room into which one entered from the pronaos was the temple proper, and contained the statue of the goddess. It was about a hundred feet long, and was hence officially called the *Hecatompedos*. The door of the small western room was on the west side of the temple. This chamber was perhaps designed for the habitation of invisible maidens who attend the maiden goddess; it is at least certain that it was called the *Parthenôn*. It is easy to imagine how a word which designated as the room of the Maidens part of the house of the Maiden, could soon come to be associated popularly with the whole building, and the name Parthenon came to mean for the ordinary ear, in defiance of official usage, the temple of Athena Parthenos, and not the chamber of her virgins.

The goddess stood in her dwelling, majestic and smiling, her colossal figure arrayed in a golden robe, a helmet on her head, her right hand holding a golden Victory, and her left resting on her shield, while the snake Erichthonius was coiled at her feet. It was a wooden statue covered with ivory and gold—ivory for the exposed flesh, gold for the raiment—and hence called *chryselephantine*. It was wrought by the Athenian sculptor of genius who has given his name to the plastic art of the Periclean age, Phidias, the son of Charmides. He had already made his fame by another beautiful statue of the goddess of the city, which the out-settlers who went forth to colonise Lemnos dedicated on the Acropolis. The Lemnian Athena was wrought in bronze and it revealed Athena to her people in the guise of their friend, while the image of the Parthenon showed her rather as their queen. Both these creations have perished, but copies have been preserved from which we can frame some far-off idea of the sculptor's work.

To Phidias too was entrusted the task of designing and carrying out those plastic decorations which were necessary to the completion of a great temple. With the metopes of the lofty entablature, from which Centaurs and Giants stood out in high relief, the great master had probably little to do. But in the two pediments and on the frieze which ran round the wall of the temple, within the colonnade, he left monuments of his genius and his skill, for mankind to adore. The triangle above the eastern portal was adorned with the scene of the birth of Athena, who has sprung from the head of Zeus, at the rising of the sun and the setting of the moon; and Iris the heavenly messenger was shown, going forth to carry the good news to the ends of the world. The pediment of the western end was occupied with the passage in the life of the goddess, that specially appertained to Attica—her triumph on the Acropolis in her contest with her rival Poseidon, for the lordship of the land. The olive which came forth from the earth by her enchantment was probably shown; and we should like to believe that at the northern and southern ends reclined the two river gods, Eridanus and Ilisus, each at the side which was nearest his own waters. The subject of the wonderful frieze which encircled the temple from end to end was the most solemn of all the ceremonies which the Athenians performed in honour of their queen. At the great Panathenaic festival, every fourth year, they went up in long procession to her temple to present her with a new robe. The advance of this procession, starting from the western side, and moving simultaneously along the northern and southern sides, to meet at the eastern entrance, was vividly shown on the frieze of the Parthenon. Walking along the peristyle and looking upwards, the spectator saw the Athenian knights—beautiful young men—on horseback, charioteers, citizens on foot, musicians, kine and sheep led for sacrifice, stately maidens with sacred vessels, the nine archons of the city, all advancing to the house of Athena where she entertains the celestials on her feast-day. The high gods are seated on thrones, Zeus on one side of Athena, Hephaestus on the other; and near the goddess is a peplos—perhaps the old peplos—in the hands of a priest. The western side of the frieze is still in its place, but the rest has been removed—the greater part to our own island.

Athena Polias had now two houses side by side on her hill. For old the old restored temple was not destroyed, nor was her old image removed from it. But in her character of Victory, yet another small habitation was built for her by the architect Callicrates, about the same time, on the bastion which the hill throws out on its southwestern side. It was an appropriate spot for the house of Victory. The Athenian standing on that platform saw Salamis and Aegina near him; his eye ranged along the Argolic coast, to the distant citadel of Corinth and the mountains of the Megarid; under the shadow of Victory he could lose himself in reveries of memory and dreams of hope. The motive of the temple, as a memorial of the Persian war, was written clear in the frieze. Whereas the sculptures of other temples of this period only alluded indirectly to that great struggle, by the representation of mythical wars—such as the war of Greek and Amazons, or of Lapiths and Centaurs, or of gods and giants; on the frieze of Athena Nike a battle between the Greeks and Persians is portrayed. It is the battle of Plataea; for Greeks are shown fighting in the Persian host.

But there were other shrines of other gods in Athens and Attica, which had been wrecked by the Persians, and which were now to be restored. From the west side of the Acropolis, as one looks down on the western quarter of the city, no building is so prominent, or called the can ever have been so prominent, as the Dorian temple of Pentelic marble which crowns the hill of Colonus, and replaced an older temple of the limestone of Piraeus. It is the temple which "the sons of Hephaestus" built for their sire, the god of handicraftsmen, who was always worshipped with special devotion at Athens—it is significant that on the frieze of the Parthenon he sits next the lady of the land. This house of Hephaestus is the only Greek temple that is not a ruin. About the same time, a marble temple of Poseidon rose on the extreme point of southern Attica, the promontory of Sunium. The Persian invasion had probably been fatal to the old temple of poros-stone. Here the sea-god, "to whom men pray at Sunium," seems to have had his own house, looking down upon his own domain; he was not forced here, as on the Acropolis, to share a sanctuary with Athena; but the goddess had a separate temple of her own hard by.

At the other extremity of the Attic land, the shrine of the goddesses of Eleusis had likewise been destroyed by the barbarians. The rebuilding had been soon begun, but, like the new temple of Athena on the Acropolis, the work had been discontinued owing to the claims of war on the revenue of the state. Under Pericles it was taken up again and completed; Ictinus made the design and Coroebus carried it out. The new Hall of Mysteries was built of the dark stone of Eleusis; one side of it was formed by the rock of the hill under which it was built; and the stone steps around the walls would have seated about 3000. As the place was close to the Megarian frontier, a strong wall with towers was erected round the precincts of the shrine; so that the place had the aspect of a fortress.

These splendid buildings required a large outlay of money, and thus gave the political opponents of Pericles a welcome handle against him. Thucydides was the leader of the outcry. He accused Pericles not merely of squandering the resources of the state which ought to be kept as a reserve for war, but of misappropriating the money of the Confederacy for purely Athenian purposes. Athens, it was said, was "like a vain woman, adorning herself with pendants of precious stones, and statues, and temples that cost a thousand talents." It is certainly true that some money was taken from the treasury of the Hellenotamiae for the new buildings, but this was only a very small part of the cost, which was mainly defrayed by the treasury of Athena and by the public treasury of Athens. There was however a good case against Pericles both on grounds of policy and on grounds of justice. The plea for taking a part of the tribute (perhaps a sixtieth—besides the sixtieth which was consecrated to Athena) doubtless was that the restoration of Greek temples destroyed by the Persians was a duty which devolved upon all the Greeks. But Pericles, with bold sophistry, argued that the allies had no reason to complain, so long as Athens defended them efficiently; this was the contract, and they had no right to interfere in her disposition of the funds. Three years after the Thirty Years' Peace, Thucydides thought that he could bring the question to an issue, and he asked the people to adjudicate by the sherd. But the people voted for the ostracism of Thucydides, and henceforward Pericles had no opponent of influence to thwart his policy or cross his way. The buildings already begun could now be continued without criticism and new works could be undertaken. A great Hall of Music or *Odeon*, intended for the musical contests which had been recently added to the Panathenaic celebrations, was now erected on the east side of the Theatre of Dionysus. Its roof, made of the masts and yard-arms of captured Persian ships, was pointed like a tent, and wits compared it to the helmet of Pericles the strategos. "The trial by sherd is over," says some one in a play which the comic poet Cratinus put on the stage at this time; "so here comes Pericles, our peak-headed Zeus, with the Odeon set on his crown."

Though Cimon, when he constructed the southern wall of the Acropolis, also built a new entrance-gate facing south-westward, it was too small and unimposing to relieve the frowning aspect of the walled hill. A more worthy approach, worthy of the Parthenon, was devised by the architect Mnesicles and met the approbation of Pericles. The buildings designed by Mnesicles occupied the whole west side of the hill. In the centre, on the brow of the height and facing westward, was to be the entrance with five gates, and on either side of this two vast columned halls—reaching to the north and south brinks of the hill—in which the Athenians could walk sheltered from sun and rain. Thrown out on the projecting cliffs in front of these halls were to be two spacious wings, flanking the ascent to the central gate. But the plan of Mnesicles took no account of the sanctuaries on the south-western part of the Acropolis, on which his new buildings would encroach. The southern colonnade would have cut short the precinct of Artemis Brauronia and the adjacent southern wing would have infringed on the enclosure of Athena Nike. On the north side there were no such impediments. The priests of these goddesses raised objections to the execution of the architect's plan at the expense of their sacred precincts, and in consequence the grand idea of Mnesicles was only partly carried out. But even after the building had been begun, Pericles and his architect never abandoned the hope that the scruples of the priests might ultimately be overcome; and, while they omitted altogether the southern colonnade and reduced the proportions of the southern wing, they built in such a way that at some future time the structure might be easily enlarged to the measures of the original design. On the northern side, too, the idea of Mnesicles was not completed, but for a different reason. The covered colonnade was never built; it was left to the last, and, when the time came, Athens was threatened by a great war, and deemed it unwise to undertake any further outlay on building. But the north-western wing was built and was adorned with paintings. The greatest paintings that Athens possessed were however not on the hill but in buildings below; and they belonged to a somewhat earlier age. It was Cimon who brought Polygnotus of Thasos to Athens, and it was when Cimon was in power that he, in collaboration with Micon, another eminent painter, decorated with life-size frescoes the new Theseum and the Anaceum, on the north side of the Acropolis, and the walls of the Painted Portico in the market-place. We have already cast a glance at the picture of the Battle of Marathon. The most famous of the pictures of the Thasian master was executed, after he had left Athens, for the speech-hall of the Cnidians at Delphi. Its subject was the underworld visited by Odysseus.

If it was vain for Athens to hope that Greece would yield her any formal acknowledgment of headship, she might at all events have the triumph of exerting intellectual influence even in the lands which were least ready to admit her claims. And in the field of art she partly fulfilled the ambition of Pericles, who, when he could not make her the queen, desired that she should be the instructress, of Hellas. When Phidias had completed the great statue of Athena in gold and ivory, and had seen it set up in the new temple, he went forth, invited by the men of Elis, to make the image for the temple of Zeus at Olympia. For five years in his workshop in the Altis the Athenian sculptor wrought at the "great chryselephantine god," and the colossal image which came from his hands was probably the highest creation ever achieved by the plastic art of Greece. The Panhellenic god, seated on a lofty throne, and clad in a golden robe, held a Victory in his right hand, a sceptre in his left. He was bearded, and his hair was wreathed with a branch of olive. Many have borne witness to the impression which the serene aspect of this manifest divinity always produced upon the heart of the beholder. "Let a man sick and weary in his soul, who has passed through many distresses and sorrows, whose pillow is unvisited by kindly sleep, stand in front of this image; he will, I deem, forget all the terrors and troubles of human life." An Athenian had wrought, for one of the two great centres of Hellenic religion, the most sublime expression of the Greek ideal of godhead. Nor was Phidias the only Athenian artist who worked abroad; we also find the architect Ictinus engaged in designing temples in the Peloponnesus.

Sect. 7. The Piraeus. Growth of Athenian Trade

The Piraeus had grown enormously since it had been fortified by Themistocles; it was now one of the great ports and cheaping-towns "in the midst of Hellas," and Pericles took in hand to make it a greater and fairer place. There was one weak point in the common defences of Piraeus and Athens. Between Munychia and the extreme end of the southern wall which ran down to the strand of Phaleron, there was an unfortified piece of marshy shore, where an enemy might land at night This defect might have been remedied by building a cross-wall, but a wholly different plan was adopted. A new long wall was built, running parallel and close to the northern wall, and, like it, joining the fortification of Piraeus with the "upper city," as Athens was locally called. The southern or Phaleron wall consequently ceased to be part of the system of defence and was allowed to fall into disrepair. Round the three harbours shipsteads were constructed, in which the vessels could lie high and dry; and on the wharfs and quays new storehouses and buildings of sundry kinds arose for the convenience of shipping and trade. On the east side of the great Harbour the chief traffic was carried on in the Place of Commerce. This mart was marked off by boundary stones, some of which are still preserved, and was subject to the control of a special board of officers. The most famous of the buildings in the Place of Commerce was the colonnade known as the Deigma or Show-place, where, merchants showed their wares. But Pericles was not content with the erection of new buildings; the whole town, which crept up the slopes of Munychia from the quays of the great Harbour, was laid out on a completely new system, which created considerable interest in Greece. It was the rectangular system, on which the main streets run parallel and are cut by cross streets at right angles. The Piraeus was the first town in Europe where this plan was adopted, which we now see carried out on a large scale in many modern cities.

The idea was due to Hippodamus, an architect of Miletus, a man of a speculative as well as practical turn, who tried with less success to apply his principles of symmetry to politics, and sketched the scheme of a model state whose institutions were as precisely correlated as the streets of his model town.

The increase of Athenian trade was largely due to the decline of the merchant cities of Ionia, a» well as to the blow which was struck to Phoenician commerce by the victory of Greece over Persia. The decay of Ionian commerce is strikingly reflected in the tribute-records of the Athenian Confederacy, where the small sums paid by the Ionians are contrasted with the larger tributes of the cities on the shores of the Propontis. Lampsacus contributes twice as much as Ephesus. Both trade and industry migrated from the eastern to the western and northern shores of the Aegean; and as this change coincided with the rise of her empire, it was Athens that it chiefly profited The population of Athens and her harbour multiplied; and about this time the whole number of the inhabitants of Attica seems to have been about 250,000—perhaps more than twice as large as the population of the Corinthian state. But nearly half of these inhabitants were slaves; for one consequence of the growth of manufactures was the inflowing of slave "hands" into the manufacturing towns. In towns where the people subsisted on the fruits of agriculture the demand for slaves remained small. It should be observed that, although Greece, and especially Athens, consumed large quantities of com brought from beyond the seas, this did not ruin the agriculture of Greece; the costs of transport were so great that home-grown corn could still be profitable.

Except in remote or unusually conservative regions, money had now entirely displaced more primitive standards of exchange and valuation. Most Greek states of any size issued their own coins, and their money at this time was in almost all cases silver. Silver had become plentiful, and prices had necessarily gone up. Thus the price of barley and wheat had become two or three times dearer than a hundred years before. Far more remarkable was the increase in the price of stock. In the days of

Solon a sheep could be bought for a drachma; in the days of Pericles, its cost might approach fifty drachmae. As money was cheap, interest should have been low; but mercantile enterprise was so active, the demand for capital so great, and security so inadequate, that the usual price of a loan was twelve per cent.

Sect. 8. Athenian Enterprise in Italy

In the far west Athens was spreading her influence and pushing her trade. She supplied Etruria with her black red-figured pottery, and there was a market for these products of her industry even in the remote valley of the Po. Her ships brought back metal-works from Tuscany, carpets and cushions from Carthage, corn, cheese and pork from Sicily. The Greek cities of Sicily had gradually adopted the Attic standard for their currency; and in the little Italian republic on the Tiber, which was afterwards destined to make laws for the whole world, the fame of the legislation of Solon was so high that envoys were sent to Athens to obtain a copy of the code. Thus Athens had stepped into the place of Chalcis; she was now the chief Ionian trader with Italian and Sicilian lands. Her rival in this western commerce was Corinth, but she was beginning to outdistance the great Dorian merchant-city. In this competition Athens had one advantage. By the possession of Naupactus she could control the entrance to the Corinthian gulf—a perpetual menace to Corinth; while the hatred which existed between Corinth and her colony Corcyra prevented this island from being as useful as it should have been to the Corinthian traffic with the west. On the other hand, Corinth had the advantage of having important colonies in the west, with which she maintained intimate relations, especially Syracuse; and these maritime cities were centres of her trade and influence. Next to Athens herself, Syracuse was probably the largest and most populous city in the Greek world. Athens had no colonies and no such centres. The disadvantage was felt by Themistocles, and his active brain devised the occupation of the site of Siris, which had been destroyed by its neighbours, but the scheme was not realised. At length the opportunity came, when Pericles was at the head of affairs; here, as in other cases, it fell upon him to execute ideas of Themistocles.

The men of old Sybaris, who since the destruction of their own town had dwelled in neighbouring cities, thought that they might at length return to build a new Sybaris on the old site; but within five years their old foes, the men of Croton, went up and drove them out. Yet they did not despair, but hoped to compass with the help of others what they had failed to accomplish by themselves. They invited Athens and Sparta to take part in founding a new city. For Sparta the offer had no attraction; but for Athens it was a welcome opportunity. The land of Sybaris was famous for its fertility, and the position was suitable for Athenian commerce. But Pericles determined to give the enterprise an international significance; it was to be more than a mere Athenian speculation. It was proclaimed throughout the Peloponnesus that whosoever wished might take part in the foundation of the new colony. The Peloponnesus—and especially Achaea, with whose cities Athens had been closely connected in recent years—was the mother country of the Greek colonies which fringed the Tarentine gulf; and the idea of Pericles was that the mother country, *under the auspices of Athens*, should establish the new city. Achaea, Arcadia, and Elis responded to the call; New Sybaris was founded; and the Athenian predominance was expressed in the image of Athena with Attic helmet on the coins of he young city.

But the men of old Sybaris were not content to stand on an equal footing with the colonists who had come to help them from the mother-country. They thought that their old connexion with the place entitled them to a privileged position; they claimed an exclusive right to the most important offices in the state. Such claims could not be tolerated; a battle was fought; and the Sybarites were driven out. But, when the city was thus deplenished, there was a pressing need for men; and for the second time an appeal was made to Athens, but this time from her own children.

To the second appeal Athens, under the guidance of Pericles, responded by an enterprise on a still greater scale. All Greece was now invited to take part in founding a Panhellenic colony. In carrying out this project the right-hand man of Pericles was the Seer and Interpreter (*Exegete*) Lampon, who was closely connected with the Eleusinian worship, and was the highest authority in Athens on all matters pertaining to religion. He obtained from the Delphic god an oracle touching the new colony; it was to be planted where men could drink water by measure and eat bread without measure. At Athens the enemies of Pericles opposed the project, and especially the Panhellenic character which he sought to impress upon it. Cratinus brought out a play deriding Lampon, and asking whether Pericles was a second Theseus who wanted to synoecize the whole of Greece. But Greece responded to the Athenian proposal, and the colony went forth under the guidance of Lampon. Not far from the site of Sybaris they found a stream gushing from a bronze pipe, which was locally known as the Bushel. Here clearly was the measured water to which the oracle pointed; while the land was so fruitful that it might well be said to furnish bread without measure. The place was named Thurii, and the new city was designed by Hippodamus, the architect who had laid out the Piraeus in rectangular streets. The constitution of Thurii was naturally a democracy; but though the influence of the Athenian model might be recognised, the colony adopted not the laws of Solon, but those of Zaleucus, the lawgiver of Locri. Some years after the foundation, the question was asked. Who was the founder? and the Delphic god himself claimed the honour. The coins of Thurii were stamped with Athena's head and an olive branch; and the place became, as it was intended, a centre of Athenian influence in Italy, although the Attic element in the population failed to maintain its predominance.

Sect. 9. Athenian Policy in Thrace and the Euxine

But Athens had greater and more immediate interests in the eastern sea where she succeeded Miletus than in the western where she succeeded Chalcis. The importance of the imports from the Pontus, especially corn, fish, and wood, was more vital than that of the wares which came to her from the west; and hence there was nothing of higher consequence in the eyes of a clear-sighted statesman than the assurance of the line of communication between Athens and the Euxine sea, and the occupation of strong and favourable points on the coasts of the Euxine itself. The outer gate of the Euxine was secured by the possession of the Chersonese which Pericles strengthened, and the inner gate by the control of Byzantium and Chalcedon, members of the Athenian Confederacy. In the Euxine, Athens relied on the Greek towns which, fringing the shores at distant intervals, looked to her for support against the neighbouring barbarians. The corn-market in the Athenian agora was sensitive to every political movement in Thrace and Scythia; and it was necessary to be ever ready to support the ships of trade by the presence of ships of war. The growth of a large Thracian kingdom under Teres and his son Sitalces demanded the attention of Athenian statesmen to these regions more pressingly than ever. The power of Teres reached to the Danube, and his influence to the Dnieper; for he married his daughter to the king of the neighbouring Scythians.

It was in order to impress the barbarians of the Euxine regions with a just sense of the greatness of the Athenian sea-power that Pericles sailed himself to the Pontus, in command of an imposing squadron. Of that voyage we know little. It is ascertained that he visited Sinope, and that in consequence of his visit the Athenians gained a permanent footing at that important point. It is probable that he also sailed to the Cimmerian Bosphorus and visited the Archaeanactid lords of Panticapaeum, who were distinguished for many a long year by their abiding friendship to Athens in her good and evil days alike. As Panticapaeum was the centre of the Euxine corn trade, this intimacy was of the highest importance.

The union of the Thracian tribes under a powerful king constrained Athens also to keep a watchful eye upon the north coast of the Aegean and the eastern frontier of Macedonia. The most important point on that coast both from a commercial and a strategic point of view was the mouth of the Strymon, where the Athenians possessed the fortress of Eion. Not far from the mouth was the bridge over which all the trade between Thrace and Macedonia passed to and fro; and up the Strymon valley ran the chief roads into the "Hinterland." The mountains of the neighbourhood were famous for the veins of gold and silver stored in their recesses; the Macedonian king Alexander had tapped a mine near Lake Prasias which yielded daily a silver talent. In the days of Cimon, Athens had attempted to strengthen Eion by establishing a colony at the Attempt to Nine Ways, by the Strymon bridge. We saw how that attempt roused the opposition of Thasos, whose interests it menaced; and, though Thasos was subdued, the colony of the Nine Ways was destroyed by the neighbouring barbarians. Thirty years later, Pericles resumed the project with greater success. Hagnon, son of Nicias, led forth a colony, of Athenians and others, and founded a new city, surrounded on three sides by the Strymon-stream, and called its name Amphipolis. It flourished and became, as was inevitable, the most important place on the coast. But a local feeling grew up unfavourable to the mother-country, and the city was lost to Athens within fifteen years of its foundation, as we shall see hereafter.

Sect. 10. The Revolt of Samos

After the ostracism of Thucydides, Pericles reigned, the undisputed leader of Athenian policy, for nearly fifteen years. He ruled as absolutely as a tyrant, and folk might have said that his rule was a continuation of the tyranny of the Pisistratids. But his position was entirely constitutional, and it had the stablest foundation, his moral influence over the sovereign people. He had the power of persuading them to do whatever he thought good, and every year for fifteen years after his rival's banishment he was elected one of the generals. Although all the ten generals nominally possessed equal powers, yet the man who possessed the supreme political influence and enjoyed the confidence of the people was practically chief of the ten and had the conduct of foreign affairs in his hands. Pericles was not irresponsible; for at the end of any official year the people could decline to re-elect him and call him to account for his actions. When he had once gained the undisputed mastery, the only forces which he used to maintain it were wisdom and eloquence. Whatever devices he may have employed in his earlier career for party purposes, he rejected now all vulgar means of courting popularity or catching votes. He believed in himself; and he sought to raise the people to his own wisdom, he would not stoop to their folly. The desire of autocratic authority was doubtless part of his nature; but his spirit was fine enough to feel that it was a greater thing to be leader of freemen whom he must convince by speech than despot of subjects who must obey his nod. Yet this leader of democracy was disdainful of the vulgar herd; and perhaps no one knew more exactly than he the weak points in a democratic constitution. There is no better equipment for the highest statesmanship than the temper which holds aloof from the public and shows a front of good-natured indifference towards unfriendly criticism; and we may be sure that this quality in the temperament of Pericles helped to establish his success and maintain his supremacy.

Pericles was a man of finer fibre than Themistocles, but he was not like Themistocles a statesman of originative genius. He originated little; he elaborated the ideas of others. He brought to perfection the sovereignty of the people which had been fully established in principle long ago; he raised to its height the empire which had been already founded. As an orator he may have had true genius; of that we cannot judge. It was his privilege to guide the policy of his country at a time when she had poets and artists who stand alone and eminent not only in her own annals and those of Greece, but in the history of mankind. The Periclean age, the age of Sophocles and Euripides, Ictinus and Phidias, was not made by Pericles. But Pericles, though not creative, was one of its most interesting figures. Perhaps his best service to Greece was one which is often overlooked: the preservation of peace for twelve years between Athens and her jealous continental neighbours— an achievement which demanded statesmanship of no ordinary tact.

In his military operations he seems to have been competent, though we have not material to criticise them minutely; he was at least generally successful. Five years after the Thirty Years' Peace, he was called upon to display his generalship. Athens was involved in a war with one of the strongest members of her Confederacy, the island of Samos. The occasion of this war was a dispute which Samos had with another member, Miletus, about the possession of Priene. It appears that Athens, some years before, had settled the constitution of Miletus and placed a garrison in the city; and yet we now find Miletus engaged in a struggle with a non-tributary ally, and, when she is worsted, appealing to Athens. The case shows how little we know of the various orderings of the relations between Athens and her allies and subjects. One would have thought the decision of such a case would have rested with Athens from the first. On the appeal, she decided in favour of Miletus, and Pericles sailed with forty-four triremes to Samos where he overthrew the aristocracy, carried away a number of hostages, and established a democratic constitution, leaving a garrison to protect it. The nobles who fled to the mainland returned one night, captured the garrison and handed them over to the Persian satrap of Sardis, with whom they were intriguing. They also recovered the hostages who had been lodged in the island of Lemnos. Athens received another blow at the same time by the revolt of Byzantium.

Pericles sailed speedily back to Samos and invested it with a large fleet. Hearing that a Phoenician squadron was coming to assist the Samians, he raised the siege and with a part of his armament went to meet it. During his absence the Samians gained some successes against the Athenian ships which were anchored close to the harbour. At the end of two weeks Pericles returned; either the Phoenicians had not appeared after all, or they had been induced to sail home. Well-nigh 200 warships now blockaded Samos, and at the end of nine months the city surrendered. The Samians undertook to pull down their walls, to surrender their ships, and pay a war indemnity which amounted to 1500 talents or thereabouts. They became subject to Athens and were obliged to furnish soldiers to her armies, but they were not made tributary.

The Athenian citizens who fell in the war received a public burial at Athens. Pericles pronounced the funeral oration, and it may have been on this occasion that he used a famous phrase of the young men who had fallen. The spring, he said, was taken out of the year.

Byzantium also came back to the confederacy. It had been a trying moment for Athens; for she had some reason to fear Peloponnesian intervention. Sparta and her allies had met to consider the situation; and the Corinthians afterwards claimed, whether truly or not, that they deprecated any interference, on the general principle that every state should be left to deal with her own rebellious allies. However the Corinthians may have acted on this occasion, it was chiefly the commercial jealousy existing between Athens and Corinth that brought on the ultimate outbreak of hostilities between the Athenians and Peloponnesians, which led to the destruction of the Athenian empire.

It seems that during the excitement of the Samian war, Pericles deemed it expedient to place some restraints upon the licence of the comic drama. What he feared was the effect which the free criticisms of the comic poets on his policy might have, not upon the Athenians themselves, but upon the strangers who were present in the theatre, and especially upon citizens of the subject states. The precaution shows that the situation was critical; though the restraints were withdrawn as soon as possible, for they were contrary to the spirit of the time. Henceforward the only check on the comic poet was that he *might* be prosecuted before the Council of Five Hundred for "doing wrong to the people," if his jests against the officers of the people went too far.

Comedy had grown up in Athens out of the mummeries of masked revellers who kept the feasts of Dionysus by singing phallic songs and flinging coarse jests at the folk. It was not till after the Persian war that the state recognised it. Then a place was given at the great festival of Dionysus to comic competitions. To the three days which were devoted to the competitions of tragedies a fourth was added for the new contest.

The comic drama then assumed form and shape. Magnes and Chionides were its first masters; but they were eclipsed by Cratinus, the most brilliant comic poet of the age of Pericles.

There is no more significant symptom of the political and social health of the Athenian state in the period of its empire, than the perfect freedom which was accorded to the comic stage, to laugh at everything in earth and heaven, and splash with ridicule every institution of the city and every movement of the day, to libel the statesmen and even jest at the gods. Such license is never permitted in an age of decadence even under the shelter of religious usage. It can only prevail in a free country where men's belief in their own strength and virtue, in the excellence of their institutions and their ideals, is still true, deep, and fervent; then they can afford to laugh at themselves. The Old Comedy is a most telling witness to the greatness of Athens.

Sect. 11. Higher Education. The Sophists

Since the days of Nestor and Odysseus, the art of persuasive speech was held in honour by the Greeks. With the rise of the democratic commonwealths it became more important, and the greater attention which was paid to the cultivation of oratory may perhaps be reflected in the introduction of a new class of proper names, which refer to excellence in addressing public assemblies. The institutions of a Greek democratic city presupposed in the average citizen the faculty of speaking in public, and for any one who was ambitious for a political career it was indispensable. If a man was hauled into a law-court by his enemies, and knew not how to speak, he was like an unarmed civilian attacked by soldiers in panoply. The power of clearly expressing ideas in such a way as to persuade an audience, was an art to be learned and taught. But it was not enough to gain command of a vocabulary; it was necessary to learn how to argue, and to exercise one's self in the discussion of political and ethical questions. There was a demand for higher education.

This tendency of democracy corresponded to the growth of that spirit of inquiry which had first revealed itself in Ionia in the field of natural philosophy. The study of nature had passed into a higher stage in the hands of two men of genius, whose speculations have had an abiding effect on science. Empedocles distinguished the "four elements," and explained the development of the universe by the forces of attraction and repulsion which have held their place till to-day in scientific theory. He also foreshadowed the doctrine of the survival of the fittest. Democritus, of Abdera, a man of vast learning, originated the atomic theory, which was in later days popularised by Epicurus, and in still later by the Roman Lucretius. The scientific imagination of Democritus generated the world from atoms, like in quality but different in size and weight, existing in void space. Such advances in the explanation of nature implied and promoted a new conception of what may be called "methodized" knowledge, and this conception was applied to every subject. The second half of the fifth century was an age of technical treatises; oratory and cookery were alike reduced to systems; political institutions and received morality became the subject of scientific inquiry. Desire of knowledge had led the Greeks to seek more information about foreign lands and peoples; they had begun both to know more of the world and to regard it with a moFC critical mind; enlightenment was spreading, prejudices were being dispelled. Herodotus, who was far from being a sceptic, fully appreciates the instructiveness of the story which he tells, how Darius asked some Greeks for what price they would be willing to eat the dead bodies of their fathers. When they cry that nothing would induce them to do so, the king calls a tribe of Indians who eat their parents, and asks them what price *they* would accept to bum the bodies of their fathers. The Indians exclaim against the bare thought of such a horror. Custom, Pindar had said and Herodotus echoes, is king of the world; and men began to distinguish between custom and nature. They felt that their own conventions and institutions required justification; the authority of usage and antiquity was not enough; and they compared human society with nature. The appeal to nature led indeed to very opposite theories. In the sight of nature, it was said, all are equal; birth and wealth are indifferent; therefore the state should be built on the basis of perfect equality. On the other hand, it was argued that in the state of nature the strong man subdues the weaker and rules over them; therefore monarchy is the natural constitution. But it matters little what particular inferences were drawn; for no attempt was made to put them into practice. The main point is that the questioning spirit was active; there were clever men everywhere, who refused to take anything on authority; who always asked, how do you know? and claimed to discuss all things in heaven and earth.

It was in this atmosphere of critical inquiry and scepticism that Greece had to provide for the higher education of her youth, which the practical conditions of the democracy demanded. The demand was met by teachers who travelled about and gave general instruction in the art of speaking and in the art of reasoning, and, out of their encyclopaedic knowledge, lectured on all possible subjects. They received fees for their course, and were called Sophists, of which name perhaps our best equivalent is "professors." Properly a sophist meant action at this famous crisis. Diodotus handled the question entirely as a matter of policy. Cleon had deprecated any appeal to the irrelevant considerations of humanity or pity; Diodotus, carefully avoiding such an appeal, deprecates on his own side with great force Cleon's appeal to considerations of justice. The Mytilenaeans have deserved the sentence of death: certainly; but the argument is entirely irrelevant. The question for Athens to consider is not what Mytilene deserves, but what it is expedient for Athens to inflict. "We are not at law with the Mytilenaeans and do not want to be told what is just; we are considering a matter of policy, and desire to know how we can turn them to account." He then goes on to argue that as a matter of fact the penalty of death is not a deterrent, and that the result of such a severe punishment will be injurious to Athens. A city which has revolted, knowing that whether she comes to terms soon or late the penalty will be the same, will never surrender; money will be wasted in a long blockade; and "when the place is taken, it will be a mere wreck."

Moreover, if the people of Mytilene, who were compelled to join with their oligarchical government in rebelling, are destroyed, the popular party will everywhere be alienated from Athens.

The reasoning of Diodotus, which was based on sound views of policy, must have confirmed many of the audience who had already been influenced by the notion of pity. But even still the Assembly was nearly equally divided, and the supporters of Diodotus won their motion by a very small majority. The ship which bore the sentence of doom had a start of about a day and a night; could it be overtaken by the trireme which was now dispatched with the reprieve? The Mytilenaean envoys supplied the crew with wine and barley, and offered large rewards if they were in time. The oarsmen continued rowing while they ate the barley, kneaded with wine and oil, and slept and rowed by turns. The first trireme, bound on an unpleasant errand, had sailed slowly. It arrived a little before the other. Paches had the decree in his hand and was about to execute it, when the second ship sailed into the harbour, and the city was saved.

The wrath of Athens against her rebellious ally was sufficiently gratified by the trial and execution of those Mytilenaeans who had been sent to Athens as especially guilty. They were perhaps about thirty in number.

Having taken away the Lesbian fleet and rased the walls of Mytilene, the Athenians divided the island, excluding Methymna, into 3000 lots of which 300 were consecrated to the gods. The rest they let to Athenian citizens as cleruchs, and the land was cultivated by the Lesbians, who paid an annual rent.

Sect. 7. Warfare in Western Greece. Tragic Events in Corcyra

While the attention of Greece was directed upon the fortunes of Plataea and Mytilene, warfare had been carried on in the regions of the west, and the reputation of the Athenian navy had risen higher. The Ambraciots had persuaded Sparta to send an expedition against Acarnania; if the Peloponnesians firmly established themselves there, they might win the whole Athenian alliance in the west. Cnemus was sent with 1000 hoplites in advance; he made an attempt on the important town of Stratus but was forced to retreat. Meanwhile a Peloponnesian fleet was to sail from Corinth to support him. It consisted of forty-seven ships, and had to pass Phormio, who was guarding the entrance of the Corinthian gulf with only twenty. Phormio let them sail into the open sea, preferring to attack them there. By skilful manoeuvres he crowded the enemy's ships into a narrow space; a morning breeze helped him by knocking the ships against one another; and when they were in confusion the Athenians dashed in and gained a complete victory. The government at Sparta could not understand how skill could gain such an advantage over far superior numbers; they sent commissioners to make an inquiry; and Cnemus was told that he must try again and be successful. A reorganised Peloponnesian fleet took up a position at Panormus in Achaea, and Phormio was stationed at Rhion on the opposite coast. The object of Cnemus was to lure or drive the enemy into the gulf where their skill in handling their ships would be less decisive than in the open sea. With this purpose he sailed towards Naupactus, and Phormio in alarm sailed along the coast to protect the place. As the Athenian ships moved near the land in single file, the enemy suddenly swung round and rowed down upon them at their utmost speed. The eleven ships which were nearest Naupactus had time to run round the right Peloponnesian wing and escape; the rest were driven aground. Twenty Peloponnesian vessels on the right were in the meantime pursuing the eleven Athenian, which were making for Naupactus. A Leucadian ship was far in advance of the others, closely pursuing an Athenian which was lagging behind. Near Naupactus a merchant vessel lay in their way, anchored in the deep water. The Athenian trireme rowed round it, struck her pursuer amidships, and sank her. This brilliant exploit startled the Peloponnesians who were coming up singing a paean of victory; the front ships dropped oars and waited for the rest. The Athenians, who had already reached Naupactus, saw the situation, and immediately bore down and gained another complete victory.

If this able admiral, Phormio, had lived, he might have extended Athenian influence considerably in western Greece. But, after a winter expedition which he made in Acarnania, he silently drops out of history, and, as we find his son Asopius sent out in the following summer at the request of the Acarnanians, we must conclude that his career had been cut short by death. Asopius made an unsuccessful attempt on Oeniadae, and was slain in a descent on Leucas. The peninsula of Leucas, and the Acarnanian Oeniadae, girt by morasses at the mouth of the river Achelous, were two main objects of Athenian enterprise in the west. Leucas was never won, but four Oeniadae, years later Oeniadae was forced to join the Athenian alliance.

Corcyra herself was to be the next scene of the war in the Ionian Sea. The prisoners whom Corinth had taken in the Epidamnian war had been released on the understanding that they were to win over Corcyra from the Athenian alliance, and their intrigues were effectual in dividing the state and producing a sanguinary revolution. The question between the Peloponnesian and the Athenian alliance was closely bound up with the cleavage between the oligarchical and the democratic party. The intriguers in the Corinthian interest and their faction formed a conspiracy to overthrow the democratic constitution. Their first step was to prosecute Peithias, the leader of the people, on the charge of scheming to make Corcyra a subject of Athens. He was acquitted, and retorted by summoning their five richest men to take their trial for cutting vine-poles in the sanctuaries of Zeus and Alcinous. They were fined a stater for each pole: such a heavy fine that the culprits sat as suppliants in the sanctuary, imploring that they might pay by instalments. The prayer was refused, and in desperation they rushed into the senate-house and slew Peithias and sixty others who were with him.

The oligarchy now had the upper hand, and they attacked the people, who fled to the acropolis and the Hyllaic harbour. The other harbour, which looks towards the mainland, along with the agora and the lower parts of the city were held by the oligarchs. Next day reinforcements came to both sides: to the people, from other parts of the island; and to the oligarchs, from the mainland. Fighting was soon resumed and the people had the advantage. In order to bar their way to the arsenal, the oligarchs set fire to the houses and buildings in the neighbourhood of the agora.

Next day twelve Athenian ships under Nicostratus arrived from Naupactus. He induced the two parties to come to an agreement, but the democrats persuaded him to leave five Athenian ships to ensure the preservation of order, for they did not trust their opponents. Nicostratus was to take five Corcyraean ships instead, and the crews of them were chosen from the oligarchs; they were in fact to be hostages for the behaviour of their fellows. But they feared they might be sent to Athens, and fled to the refuge of a temple. Nicostratus could not induce them to stir. The people regarded this distrust as a proof of criminal designs, and armed anew. The rest of the oligarchs then fled to the temple of Hera, but the democrats induced them to cross over to an islet off the coast.

Four or five days later a Peloponnesian fleet of fifty-three ships arrived under Alcidas, who had just returned from his expedition to Ionia. In a naval engagement outside the harbour the Corcyraeans fought badly, and the Athenians were forced to retreat; but the Peloponnesians did not follow up their success, and soon afterwards, hearing that an Athenian armament of sixty ships was on its way, returned home.

The democratic party was now in a position to wreak vengeance on its foes, who had gratuitously disturbed the peace of the city and sought to submit it to the yoke of its ancient enemy. The most vindictive and inhuman passions had been roused in the people by the attempt of the oligarchs on their liberty, and they now gave vent to these passions without regard to honour or policy. The 400 suppliants had returned from the island, and were again under the protection of Hera. Fifty of them were persuaded to come forth to take their trial, and were executed. The rest, seeing their fate, aided each other in committing suicide; some hung themselves on the trees in the sacred enclosure. Eurymedon arrived with the Athenian fleet and remained seven days. During this time, the Corcyraeans slew all whom they suspected of being opposed to the democracy, and many victims were sacrificed to private enmity. "Every form of death was to be seen, and everything, and more than everything that commonly happens in revolutions, happened then. The father slew the son, and the suppliants were torn from the temples and slain near them; some of them were even walled up in the temple of Dionysus and there perished. To such extremes of cruelty did revolution go; and this seemed to be the worst of revolutions because it was the first." Eurymedon looked on and did not intervene.

While the democracy cannot be excused for the se horrible excesses, the fact remains that the guilt of causing the revolution rests entirely with the oligarchs. The chief victims of the democratic fury deserve small compassion; they had set the example of violence. The occurrences at Corcyra made a profound impression in Greece, reflected in the pages of Thucydides. That historian has used the episode as the text for deep comments on the revolutionary spirit which soon began to disturb the states of the Greek world. Party divisions were encouraged and aggravated by the hope or fear of foreign intervention, the oligarchs looking to the Lacedaemonians, and the democrats to the Athenians. In time of peace these party struggles would have been far less bitter. This acute observation is illustrated by a famous modern instance, the French Revolution, where the worst outrages of the revolutionists were provoked by foreign intervention. In that great Revolution too we can verify the Greek historian's analysis of the effect of the revolutionary spirit, when it runs wild, on the moral nature of men. The revolutionists "determined to outdo the report of all who had preceded them by the ingenuity of their enterprises and the activity of their revenges. The meaning of words had no longer the same relation to things, but was changed by them as they thought proper. Reckless daring was held to be loyal courage; prudent delay was the excuse of a coward; moderation was the disguise of unmanly weakness; to know everything was to do nothing. Frantic energy was the true quality of a man. The lover of violence was always trusted and his opponent suspected." It was dangerous to be quiet and neutral. "The citizens who were of neither party fell a prey to both; either they were disliked because they held aloof, or men were jealous of their surviving." The laws of heaven as well of civilised societies were set aside without scruple amid the impatience of party spirit, the zeal of contention, the eagerness of ambition, and the cravings of revenge. These are some of the features in the delineation which Thucydides has drawn of the diseased condition of political life in the city-states of Greece.

But the sequel of the Corcyraean revolution has still to be recorded. About 600 of the oligarchs who escaped the vengeance of their opponents established themselves on Mount Istone in the north-east of the island, and easily becoming masters of the open country they harassed the inhabitants of the city for two years. Then an Athenian fleet, of which the ultimate destination was Sicily, under the command of Eurymedon and Sophocles, arrived at Corcyra; and the Athenians helped the democrats to storm the fort on Mount Istone. The oligarchs capitulated on condition that the Athenian people should determine how they were to be dealt with. The generals placed them in the island of Ptychia, on the understanding that, if any of their number attempted to escape, all should be deprived of the benefit of the previous agreement. But the democrats apprehended that the prisoners would not be put to death at Athens, and they were determined that their enemies should die. A foul trick was planned and carried out. Friends of the prisoners were sent over to the island, who said that the generals had resolved to leave them to the mercy of the democrats, and advised them to escape, offering to provide a ship. A few of the captives fell into the trap and were caught starting. All the prisoners were immediately handed over to the Corcyraeans, who shut them up in a large building. They were taken out in batches of twenty, and made to march, tied together, down an avenue of hoplites, who smote and wounded any whom they recognised as a personal enemy. Three batches had thus marched to execution, when their comrades in the building, who thought they were merely being removed to another prison, discovered the truth. They called on the Athenians, but they called in vain. Then they refused to stir out of the building or let any one enter. The Corcyraeans did not attempt to force their way in. They tore off the roof, and hurled bricks and shot arrows from above. The captives, absolutely helpless, began to anticipate the purpose of their tormentors by taking their own lives, piercing their throats with the arrows which were shot down, or strangling themselves with the ropes of some beds which were in the place or with strips of their own dress. The work of destruction went on during the greater part of the night; all was over when the day dawned; and the corpses were carried outside the city. Thus ended the Corcyraean revolution, and the last scene was more ghastly even than the first. Eurymedon had less excuse, on this occasion, for refusing to intervene than he had two years before; since the prisoners had surrendered to the Athenians. It was said that he and Sophocles were ready to take advantage of the base trick of the democrats, because, unable to take the captives to Athens themselves, being bound for Sicily, they could not bear that the credit should fall to another. The oligarchical faction at Corcyra was now utterly annihilated, and the democrats lived in peace.

Sect. 8. Campaigns of Demosthenes in the West

During the Corcyraean troubles, the war had not rested in western Greece. An Athenian fleet under the general Demosthenes had sailed round the Peloponnesus and attacked the "island" of Leucas. Demosthenes was an enterprising commander, distinguished from most of his fellows by a certain originality of conception. On this occasion, the idea of making a great stroke induced him to abandon the operations at Leucas,—though the Acarnanians thought he might have taken the town by blockade,—and engage in a new enterprise on the north of the Corinthian gulf. Most of the lands between Boeotia and the western sea—Phocis, Locris, Acarnania—were friendly to Athens. But the hostility of the uncivilised Aetolians rendered land operations in those regions dangerous. Demosthenes conceived the plan of reducing the Aetolians, so that he could then operate from the west on Doris and Boeotia, without the danger of his communications being threatened in the rear. His idea, in fact, was to bring the Corinthian gulf into touch with the Euboean sea. The Spartans, it is to be observed, were at this very time concerning themselves with the regions of Mount Oeta. The appeals of Doris on the south, and Trachis on the north, of the Oetaean range, for protection against the hostilities of the mountain tribes, induced the Lacedaemonians to send out a colony, which was established in Trachis not very far from the Pass of Thermopylae, under the name of Heraclea. A colony was an unusual enterprise for Sparta; but Heraclea had a more important significance and intention than the mere defence of members of the amphictiony. It was a place from which Euboea could be attacked; and it might prove of the greatest service, as an intermediate station, for carrying on operations in the Chalcidic peninsula. The fears which the foundation of Heraclea excited at Athens were indeed disappointed; Heraclea never flourished; it was incessantly assailed by the powerful hostility of the Thessalians, and its ruin was completed by the flagrantly unjust administration of the Lacedaemonian governors. But its first foundation was a serious event; and it seems highly probable that Demosthenes, when he formed his plan, had before his mind the idea of threatening Heraclea from the south by the occupation of Doris. But his plan, attractive as it might sound, was eminently impracticable. The preliminary condition was the subjugation of a mountainous country, involving a warfare in which Demosthenes was inexperienced and hoplites were at a great disadvantage. The Messenians of Naupactus represented to him that Aetolia, a land of unwalled villages, could easily be reduced. But the Messenians had their own game to play. They suffered from the hostilities of their Aetolian neighbours and wanted to use the ambition of the Athenian general for their own purpose.

 The Acarnanians, who were deeply interested in the defeat of Leucas, were indignant with Demosthenes for not prosecuting the blockade and refused to join him against Aetolia. Starting from Oeneon in Locris, the Athenians and some allies—not a large force—advanced into the country, hoping to reduce several tribes before they had time to combine. But the Aetolians had already learned his plans, and were already collecting a great force. The main chance of Demosthenes lay in the co-operation of the Ozolian Locrians, who knew the Aetolian country and mode of warfare and were armed in the Aetolian fashion. Demosthenes committed the error of not waiting for them. He was consequently unable to deal with the Aetolian javelin-men. At Aegition, rushing down from the hills they wrought havoc among the invaders who had captured the town. A hundred and twenty Athenian hoplites fell—"the very finest men whom the city of Athens lost during the war." Demosthenes did not dare to return to Athens. He remained at Naupactus, and soon had an opportunity of retrieving his fame.

The Lacedaemonians answered this invasion of Aetolia by sending 3000 hoplites under Eurylochus against Naupactus. Five, hundred of these troops came from Heraclea, the newly-founded colony. Naupactus, ill-defended, was barely saved by the energy of Demosthenes, who persuaded the Acarnanians to send reinforcements. Eurylochus abandoned the siege, and withdrew to the neighbourhood of Calydon and Pleuron in southern Aetolia, for the purpose of joining the Ambraciots in an attack upon Argos. Winter had begun when the Ambraciots descended from the north into the Argive territory and seized the fort of Olpae, which stands, a little north of Argos, on a hill by the sea, and was once used as a hall of justice by the Acarnanian league. Demosthenes was asked by the Acarnanians to be their leader in resisting this attack, and a message for help was sent to twenty Athenian vessels which were coasting off the Peloponnesus. The troops of Eurylochus marched from the south across Acarnania and joined their allies at Olpae. The Athenian ships arrived in the Ambracian gulf, and, with the reinforcements which they brought, Demosthenes gave battle to the enemy between Olpae and Argos, and by a skilfully contrived ambuscade annulled the advantage which they had in superior numbers. Eurylochus was slain, and the Peloponnesians delivered themselves from their perilous position—between Argos and the Athenian ships—by making a secret treaty with Demosthenes, in which the Ambraciots were not included. It was arranged that they should retreat stealthily without explaining their intention to the Ambraciots. It was good policy on the part of Demosthenes; for by this treacherous act the Lacedaemonians would lose their character in that part of Greece. The Peloponnesians crept out of Olpae one by one, pretending to gather herbs and sticks. As they got farther away, they stepped out more quickly, and then the Ambraciots saw what was happening and ran out to overtake them. The Acarnanians slew about 200 Ambraciots, and the Peloponnesians escaped into the land of Agraea. But a heavier blow was in store for Ambracia. Reinforcements of that city, ignorant of the battle, were coming to Olpae. Demosthenes sent forward some of his troops to lie in ambush on their line of march. At Idomene, some miles north of Olpae, there are two peaks of unequal height. The higher was seized in advance by the men of Demosthenes; the Ambraciots when they arrived encamped on the lower. Demosthenes then advanced with the rest of his troops and attacked the enemy at dawn, when they were still half asleep. Most were slain, and those who escaped at first found the mountain paths occupied. Thucydides says that during the first ten years of the war "no such calamity happened within so few days to any Hellenic state," and he does not give the numbers of those who perished, because they would appear incredible in proportion to the size of the state. Demosthenes might have captured the city if he had pushed on, but the Acarnanians did not desire a permanent Athenian occupation at their doors; they were content that their neighbour was rendered harmless. A treaty of alliance for 100 years was concluded between the Acarnanians, with the Amphilochians of Argos, and the Ambraciots. Neither side was to be required by the other to join against its own allies in the great war, but they were to help each other to defend their territories. Some time afterwards Anactorion, and then Oeniadae, were won over to the Athenian alliance.

Sect. 9. Nicias and Cleon. Politics at Athens

The success against Ambracia compensated for the failure in Aetolia, and Demosthenes could now return to Athens. His dashing style of warfare and his bold plans must have caused grave mistrust among the older, more experienced, and more commonplace commanders. Nicias, the son of Niceratus, who seems to have already won, without deserving, the chief place as a military authority at Athens, must have shaken his head over the doings of Demosthenes in the west. Nicias, a wealthy conservative slave-owner, who speculated in the silver-mines of Laurion, was one of the mainstays of that party which was out of sympathy with the intellectual and political progress of Athens, and bitterly opposed to the new politicians like Cleon who wielded the chief influence in the Assembly.

The ability of Nicias was irretrievably mediocre; he would have been an excellent subordinate officer, but he had not the qualities of a leader or a statesman. Yet he possessed a solid and abiding influence at Athens, through his impregnable respectability, his superiority to bribes, and his scrupulous superstition, as well as his acquaintance with the details of military affairs. This homage paid to mediocre respectability throws light on the character of the Athenian democracy, and the strength of the conservative party. Nicias belonged to the advocates of peace and was well-disposed to Sparta, so that for several reasons he might be regarded as a successor to Cimon. But his political opponents, though they constantly defeated him on particular measures, never permanently undermined his influence. He understood the political value of gratifying in small ways those prejudices of his fellow-citizens which he shared himself; and he spared no expense in the religious service of the state. As Thucydides says, he thought too much of divination and omens. He had an opportunity of displaying his religious devotion and his liberality on the occasion of the purification of the island of Delos, which was probably undertaken to induce Apollo to stay the plague. The dead were removed from all the tombs, and it was ordained that henceforth no one should die or give birth to a child on the sacred island. Those who were near to either should cross over to Rheneia. The Athenians revived in a new form the old festival, celebrated in the Homeric hymn to Apollo, the festival to which "the long-robed Ionians gathered, and made thee glad, O Phoebus, with boxing, dancing, and song." The games were restored, and horse-races introduced for the first time. Four years later the purification was perfected by the removal of all the inhabitants, and the Persians accorded them a refuge at Adramyttion.

Conducting such ceremonies, Nicias was in his right place. Unfortunately such excellence had an undue weight; and it should be noted that this is one of the drawbacks of a city-state. In a large modern state, the private life and personal opinions of a statesman have small importance and are not weighed by his fellow-countrymen in the scale against his political ability, save in rare exceptional cases. But in a small city the statesman's private life is always before men's eyes, and his political position is distinctly affected, according as he shocks or gratifies their prejudices and predilections. A mediocre man is able, by judicious conforming, to attain an authority to which his brains give him no claim. Pericles was indeed so strong that his influence could survive attacks on his morality and his orthodoxy. Nicias maintained his position because he never shocked the public sense of decorum and religion by associating with an Aspasia or an Anaxagoras. The Athenian people combined in a remarkable degree the capacity of appreciating both respectability and intellectual power; their progressive instinct was often defeated by conservative prejudices.

Though Nicias was one of those Athenians who were not in full sympathy with the policy of Pericles and approved still less of the policy of his successors, he was thoroughly loyal to the democracy. But an oligarchical party still existed, secretly active, and always hoping for an opportunity to upset the democratic constitution. This party, or a section of it, seems to have been known at this time as the "Young

Party." It included, among others who will appear on the stage of history some years later, the orator Antiphon, who was now coming into public notice in connexion with some sensational lawsuits. Against the dark designs of this party, as well as against the misconduct of generals, Cleon was constantly on the watch; he could describe himself in the Assembly as the "people's watch-dog." But at present these oligarchs were harmless; so long as no disaster from without befell Athens, they had no chance; all they could do was to make common cause with the other enemies of Cleon, and air their discontent in anonymous political pamphlets. Chance has preserved us a work of this kind, written in one of these years by an Athenian of oligarchical views. Its subject is the Athenian democracy, and the writer professes to answer on behalf of the Athenians the criticisms which the rest of the Greeks pass on Athenian institutions. "I do not like democracy myself," he says; "but I will show that from their point of view the Athenians manage their state wisely and in the manner most conducive to the interests of democracy." The defence is for the most part a veiled indictment; it displays remarkable acuteness, with occasional triviality. The writer has grasped and taken to heart one deep truth, the close connexion of the sea-power of Athens with its advanced democracy. It is just, he remarks, that the poor and the common folk should have more influence than the noble and rich; for it is the common folk that row the ships and make the city powerful, not the hoplites and the well-born and the worthy. Highly interesting is his observation that slaves and metics enjoyed what he considered unreasonable freedom and immunity at Athens: "Why, you may not strike one of them, nor will a slave make way for you in the street." And his malicious explanation is interesting too; the common folk dress so badly that you might easily mistake one of them for a slave or a metic, and then there would be a to-do if you struck a citizen. There is perhaps a touch of malice, too, in the statement that the commercial empire of Athens, which brought to her wharfs the delicacies of the world, was affecting her language, as well as her habits of life, and filling it with foreign words.

An important feature in the political history of Athens in these years was the divorce of the military command from the leadership in the Assembly, and the want of harmony between the chief Strategoi and the Leaders of the People. The tradesmen who swayed the Assembly had no military training or capacity, and they were always at a disadvantage when opposed by men who spoke with the authority of a strategos on questions of military policy. Until recent years the post of General had been practically confined to men of property and good family. But a change ensued, perhaps soon after the death of Pericles, and men of the people were elected. The comic poet Eupolis, in a play called the *Demes*—in which the great leaders, Miltiades and Themistocles, Aristides and Pericles, are summoned back to life that they may see and deplore degenerate Athens—meditates thus on the contrast between latter-day generals and their predecessors:

> Men of lineage fair
> And of wealthy estate
> Once our generals were,
> The noble and great,
>
> Whom as gods we adored, and as gods they guided and guarded the state.
>
> Things are not as then.
> Ah, how different far
> A manner of men
> Our new generals are.
>
> The rascals and refuse our city now chooses to lead us to war!

Cleon was a man of brains and resolution. He was ambitious to rule the state as Pericles had ruled it; and for this purpose he saw clearly that he must gain triumphs in the field as well as in the Assembly. Hitherto his main activity had been in the law-courts, where he called officers to account and maintained the safeguards of popular government. If he was to be more than an opposition leader, occasionally forcing measures through the Assembly, if he was to exercise a permanent influence on the administration, he must be ready, when a good opportunity offered, to undertake the post of strategos; and, supported by the experience of an able colleague, he need not disgrace himself. An understanding, therefore, between Cleon and the enterprising Demosthenes was one which seemed to offer advantages to both; acting together they might damage both the political and the military position of Nicias.

But before we pass to a famous enterprise, which was probably from the result of such an understanding, we must note the great cost which the continuation of the war entailed. It was found necessary to borrow from the temple treasures, at a nominal interest, to defray the military expenses. But this was not enough. The financiers of Athens—and Cleon must probably bear a large share of the responsibility—induced the people to raise the tribute of the subject states. If the tribute was not doubled, it was very nearly doubled; the total amount, at the lowest estimate, did not fall far short of 1000 talents. We possess considerable fragments of the stone on which this assessment was written; it is a monument of the injustice of a democracy blinded by imperial ambition against which Thucydides son of Melesias had protested at an earlier stage. But at this stage, the raising of the tribute was a necessity; Athens could not retreat. There were indeed still men, especially among the Young Party, to lift up a voice on behalf of the Cities; and the glaring injustice of the position of Athens was smartly ridiculed by Aristophanes, who ironically suggested in one of his comedies that if the Cities were compelled to do their duty, each would enable twenty Athenians to live in idleness on the fat of the land, "on hare and beestings pudding."

It may seem strange to find that in a time of financial pressure, when it was necessary not only to introduce an extraordinary tax on property but to afflict the allies with heavier burdens, Athens saw fit to increase her domestic expenditure. One of Cleon's most important measures was the raising of the judges' fee from one obol, at which it had been fixed by Pericles, to three obols. It would be a mistake to consider this measure a mere bid for popularity. We shall hardly be wrong in regarding it as an attempt to relieve the distress which the yearly invasions of Attica and losses of the harvests inflicted upon the poorer citizens.

Sect. 10. The Athenian Capture of Pylos

It was doubtless through the influence of Cleon that Demosthenes, though he received no official command, was sent to accompany the fleet of forty ships which was now ready to start for the west, under Eurymedon and Sophocles. We have already seen this fleet at Corcyra assisting the People against the oligarchical exiles who had established themselves on Mount Istone. Demosthenes accompanied the expedition without any official command. He had a plan in his head for establishing a military post in the western Peloponnesus; and he was allowed to take advantage of the sailing of the fleet and use it according to his discretion. Arriving off the coast of Messenia, Demosthenes asked the commanders to put in at Pylos, but they had heard that the Peloponnesian fleet had already reached Corcyra, and demurred to any delay. But chance favoured the design of Demosthenes. Stress of weather drove them into the harbour of Pylos, and then Demosthenes pressed them to fortify the place. The task was easy; for the place was naturally strong and there was an abundance of material, stone and timber, at hand. The commanders ridiculed the idea. "There are many other desert promontories in the Peloponnesus," they said, "if you want to waste the money of the city." But the stormy weather detained the ships; the soldiers were idle; and at length, for the sake of something to do, they adopted the project of Demosthenes and fell to the work of fortifying Pylos.

The features of the scene, which was now to become illustrious by a striking military episode, must be clearly grasped. The high promontory of Pylos or Coryphasion was on three sides encompassed by water. Once it had been an island, but at this time it was connected with the mainland on the north side by a low sand-bar. If we go further back into prehistoric days, Pylos had been part of a continuous line of coast-cliff. In this line three rents were made, which admitted the sea behind the cliff and isolated the islands of Pylos and Sphacteria. Accumulation of sand gradually covered the most northern breach and reunited Pylos with the mainland, but the other openings were never filled up and Sphacteria still remains an island. Originally Pylos and Sphacteria, when they had been severed, formed the sea-wall of one great landlocked bay; but a curving sand-bar has gradually been formed, which now joins the mainland with the southern extremity of Pylos, and secludes a small lagoon of which Pylos forms the western side. It is impossible to say whether the formation of this sand-bar had perceptibly begun in the time of Demosthenes; but in any case it seems probable that it had not advanced so far as to hinder the waters behind Pylos from appearing to be part of a continuous bay. This north corner of the bay—now a marshy lagoon—was sheltered and afforded harbourage for ships; the rest of the bay—the modern bay of Navarino—had no good anchorage; but the whole sheet of water, by virtue of the northern corner, was called a harbour. It follows from what has been said that there were two entrances into the bay: the narrow water which divides Pylos from Sphacteria, and the wide passage which severs the southern point of Sphacteria from the opposite mainland. We must distinguish yet another smaller bay on the north side of the Pylos hill. The sand-bar which there connects Pylos with the mainland is of lunar shape and forms the little circular basin of Buphras, dominated by the height of Pylos on the south and a far lower, nameless hill on the north.

The length of Pylos is less than a mile. On the sea-side it was hard to land, and the harbour side was strongly protected by steep Pylos cliffs. Only in three places was it found necessary to build walls: (1) at the south-east corner, where the cliffs slope down to the channel for about 100 yards; (2) along the shore on the south-west side close to the entrance to the bay, for four or five hundred yards; (3) the northern defence of the position consisted of a line of land cliffs, which required no artificial fortification except at the western extremity, where they decline before they reach the sea; here another wall was built. One of the soldiers present vividly described to Thucydides the manner in which the fortifications were wrought. Being unprovided with iron tools they brought stones which they picked out, and put them together as they happened to fit; if they required to use mortar, having no hods, they carried it on their backs, which they bent so as to form a resting-place for it, clasping their hands behind them that it might not fall off.^ In six days the work was finished, and the fleet went on its way, leaving Demosthenes with five ships to hold Pylos.

The Lacedaemonian army under Agis had invaded Attica earlier than usual, before the corn was ripe. Want of food, wet weather, and then perhaps the news from Pylos, decided them to return to Sparta after a sojourn of only two weeks within the Attic borders. They did not proceed immediately to Pylos, but another body of Spartans was sent on; requisitions for help were dispatched to the Peloponnesian allies; and the sixty ships at Corcyra were hastily summoned. These ships succeeded in eluding the notice of the Athenian fleet which had now reached Zacynthus. In the meantime Demosthenes, beset by the Spartan troops, sent two of his ships to overtake the fleet and beg Eurymedon to return to succour him.

The object of the Lacedaemonians was to blockade the hill of Pylos by land and sea, and to prevent Athenian succours from landing. They probably established their camp on the north side of Pylos, so that no ships entering the bay of Buphras could bring help to the fort. They were moreover afraid that the Athenians might use the island of Sphacteria as a basis for military operations, and accordingly Epitadas occupied Sphacteria with 420 Spartans and their attendant Helots. It would have been easy to block the narrow entrance to the bay between Pylos and the island; but there was little use in doing so, as the Athenian ships would be able to enter by the ingress at the south of the island, a passage about three-quarters of a mile wide—far too wide to block with so small a fleet.

The Lacedaemonians then prepared to attack the place, before help could come to the Athenians. Demosthenes posted the greater part of his force to guard the northern line of defence and the southeastern corner; while he himself with sixty hoplites and some archers took his stand on the edge of the south-western shore, which though rocky and perilous was the spot where the enemy had the best prospect of effecting a landing. Thrasymelidas was the name of the Spartan admiral. He had forty-three ships, which he brought up in relays, the crews fighting and resting by turns. The great danger was that of running the vessels on reefs. Brasidas who commanded one of the ships was the leading spirit. "Be not sparing of timber," he cried to those who seemed to draw back from the rocks; "the enemy has built a fortress in your country. Perish the ships, and force a landing." But in trying to disembark he was wounded and lost his shield. It was washed ashore and set up in the trophy which the Athenians afterwards erected. The Spartan attack which was renewed on two subsequent days was repelled. It was a singular turn of fortune, says Thucydides,^ which drove the Athenians to repel the Lacedaemonians, who were attacking them by sea from the Lacedaemonian coast, and the Lacedaemonians to fight for a landing on their own soil, now hostile to them, in the face of the Athenians. For in those days it was the great glory of the Lacedaemonians to be an inland people distinguished for their military prowess, and of the Athenians to be a nation of sailors and the first naval power in Hellas.

The fleet from Zacynthus, now augmented to fifty ships by some reinforcements, at length arrived. But finding the shores of the bay of Buphras and the island of Sphacteria occupied, they withdrew for the night to the isle of Prote which was some miles distant. The next morning they returned, determined to sail into the harbour, if the enemy did not come out to meet them. The Lacedaemonians were preparing their ships for action, evidently intending to fight in the bay. The Athenians therefore rowed in by both entrances; some of the enemy's vessels which were able to come out to meet them were captured; and a tremendous struggle ensued close to the shore. The Athenians were tying the empty beached ships to their own and endeavouring to drag them away, the Lacedaemonians dashed into the sea and were pulling them back. The Lacedaemonians knew that, if they lost their ships, the party on the island of Sphacteria would be cut off. Most of the empty ships were saved; but the fleet was so far damaged and outnumbered that the Athenians were able to blockade Sphacteria.

The interest of the story now passes from Pylos to Sphacteria. The blockade of Demosthenes and his Athenians in Pylos by the Spartans has changed into a blockade of Epitadas and his Spartans in Sphacteria by the Athenians. The tidings of this change in the situation caused grave alarm at Sparta and some of the ephors came themselves to see what measures could be taken. They decided that nothing could be done for the relief of the island, and obtained from the Athenian generals a truce for the purpose of sending ambassadors to Athens to ask for peace. The terms of this truce were as follows:

The Lacedaemonians shall deliver into the hands of the Athenians at Pylos the ships in which they fought, and shall also bring thither and deliver over any other ships of war which are in Laconia; and they shall make no assault upon the fort either by sea or land. The Athenians shall permit the Lacedaemonians on the mainland to send to those on the island a fixed quantity of kneaded flour, viz. two Attic quarts of barleymeal for each man, and a pint of wine, and also a piece of meat; for an attendant half these quantities; they shall send them into the island under the inspection of the Athenians, and no vessel shall sail in by stealth. The Athenians shall guard the island as before, but not land, and shall not attack the Peloponnesian forces by land or sea. If either party violate this agreement in any particular, however slight, the truce is to be at an end. The agreement is to last until the Lacedaemonian ambassadors return from Athens, and the Athenians are to convey them thither and bring them back in a trireme. When they return, the truce is to lie at an end, and the Athenians are to restore the ships in the same condition in which they received them.

In accordance with these terms, sixty ships were handed over and the ambassadors went to Athens. They professed the readiness of

Sparta to make peace and pleaded for generous treatment on the part of Athens. At heart most of the Athenians were probably desirous of peace. But the Assembly was under the influence of Cleon, and he, as the opponent of Nicias and the peace-party, urged the Athenians to propose terms which could hardly be accepted. It might seem indeed an exceptionally favourable moment to attempt to undo the humiliation of the Thirty Years' Truce, and win back some of the possessions which had been lost twenty years ago. Not only Nisaea and Pagae, the harbours of the Megarid, but Achaea and Troezen, were demanded as the purchase of the lives of the Spartans in Sphacteria. The embassy returned to Pylos disappointed, and the truce came to an end. But the Athenians refused to give back the sixty ships, on the pretext of some slight infraction of the truce on the part of the Lacedaemonians.

The blockade proved a larger and more difficult matter than the Athenians had hoped. Reinforced by twenty more triremes from Athens, they lay round the island, both in the bay, and, except when the wind was too high, on the seaside; and two ships kept continually cruising round in opposite directions. But their vigilance was eluded, and Sphacteria was secretly supplied with provisions. Large sums were offered to any who succeeded in conveying meal, wine, or cheese to the island; and Helots, who did such service, were rewarded with freedom. When a strong wind from the west or north drove the Athenian ships into the bay, the daring crews of provision-boats beat recklessly into the difficult landing-places on the seaside. Moreover some skilful divers managed to reach the shores of the island,—drawing skins with poppy-seed mixed with honey, and pounded linseed. But this device was soon discovered and prevented.

And besides the difficulty of rendering the blockade complete in a high wind, the maintenance of it was extremely unpleasant. As there was no proper anchorage, the crews were obliged to take their meals on land by turns,—generally in the south part of Sphacteria, which was not occupied by the Spartans. And they depended for their supply of water on one well, which was in the fort of Pylos. The supply of food was deficient,—for it had to be conveyed round the Peloponnesus. At home the Athenians were disappointed at the protraction of the siege, and grew impatient. They were sorry that they had declined the overtures of the Lacedaemonians, and there was a reaction of feeling against Cleon. That statesman took the bold course of denying the reports from Pylos, and said—with a pointed allusion to the strategos Nicias—that if the Generals were men they would sail to the island and capture the garrison. "If I were commander," he added, "I would do it myself." The scene which follows is described in one of the rare passages where the most reserved of all historians condescends to display a little personal animosity. Seeing that the people were murmuring at Cleon, Nicias stood up and offered, on the part of his colleagues, to give Cleon any force he asked for and let him try. Cleon—says Thucydides—at first imagined that the offer of Nicias was only a pretence and was willing to go; but finding that he was in earnest, he tried to back out and said that not he but Nicias was general. He was now alarmed, for he never imagined that Nicias would go so far as to give up his place to him. Again Nicias bade him take the command of the expedition against Pylos, which he formally gave up to him in the presence of the Assembly. And the more Cleon declined the proffered command and tried to retract what he had said, so much the more the multitude, as their manner is, urged Nicias to resign and shouted to Cleon that he should sail. At length, not knowing how to escape from his own words, he undertook the expedition and, coming forward, said that he was not afraid of the Lacedaemonians and that he would sail without withdrawing a single man from the city, if he were allowed to have the Lemnian and Imbrian forces now at Athens, the auxiliaries from Aenus who were targeteers, and four hundred archers from other places. With these and with the troops already at Pylos he gave his word that he would either bring the Lacedaemonians alive or kill them on the spot. His vain words moved the Athenians to laughter; nevertheless the wiser sort of men were pleased when they reflected that of two good things they could not fail to obtain one—either there would be an end of Cleon, which they would have greatly preferred, or, if they were disappointed, he would put the Lacedaemonians into their hands.

The story is almost too good to be true. But whether Cleon desired the command or had it thrust upon him against his will, his words which moved the Athenians to laughter were fully approved by the event. He chose Demosthenes as his colleague; and, invested with the command by a formal vote of the Assembly, he immediately set sail.

In the meantime Demosthenes, wishing like Cleon to bring matters to an issue, was meditating an attack upon Sphacteria. This desert island is about two miles and three-quarters long. At the northern extremity rises a height, higher than the acropolis of Pylos over against it, and on the east side descending, a sheer cliff, into the water of the bay. Some of the Spartans had naturally occupied the summit, but the chief encampment of their small force was in the centre of the island, close to the only well; and an outpost was set on a hill farther to the south. An assault was difficult not only because the landing-places on both sides were bad, but because the island was covered with close bush, which gave the Spartans who knew the ground a great advantage. Demosthenes had experienced in Aetolia the difficulties of fighting in a wood. But one day, when some Athenians were taking their noonday meal on the south shore of the island, the wood was accidentally kindled, and, a wind arising, the greater part of the bush was burnt. It was then possible to see more clearly the position and the numbers of the Lacedaemonians, and, when Cleon arrived, the plan of attack was matured. Embarking at night all their hoplites in a few ships, forces land Cleon and Demosthenes landed before dawn on the south of the island, partly on the seaside and partly on the harbour side, near the spot where the Lacedaemonians had their outpost. The whole number of troops that landed must have been nearly 14,000, against which the Spartans had only 420 hoplites and perhaps as many Helots. And yet a high military authority described the Athenian enterprise as mad. The truth seems to be that it could hardly have succeeded if the Spartan commander had disposed his forces to the best advantage, posting watches at all possible landing-places and organising a proper system of signals.

The outpost was at once overpowered, and light-armed troops advanced towards the main Spartan encampment, along a high ridge on the harbour side of the island. Others moved along the low shore on the seaside; so that when the main body of the Spartans saw their outpost cut to pieces and began to move southward against the Athenian hoplites, they were harassed on either side by the archers and targeteers, whom, encumbered by their arms and in difficult ground, they were unable to pursue. And the attacks of these light-armed troops, as they grew more fully conscious of their own superiority in numbers and saw that their enemy was growing weary, became more formidable. Clouds of dust arose from the newly burnt wood—so Thucydides reports the scene from the vivid description of an eye-witness—and there was no possibility of a man's seeing what was before him, owing to the showers of arrows and stones hurled by their assailants which were flying amid the dust And now the Lacedaemonians began to be sorely distressed, for their felt cuirasses did not protect them against the arrows, and the points of the javelins broke off where they struck them. They were at their wits' end, not being able to see out of their eyes or to hear the word of command, which was drowned by the cries of the enemy. Destruction was staring them in the face, and they had no means or hope of deliverance.

At length it was determined that the only chance lay in retreating to the high hill at the north of the island. About a mile had to be traversed to the foot of the hill; but the ground was very difficult. The endurance and discipline of the Spartan soldiers was conspicuously displayed in this slow retreat which was accomplished, with but a small loss, under a burning sun, by men who were suffering from thirst and weary with the distress of an unequal battle. When they had reached and climbed the hill the battle assumed another aspect. On the high ground, no longer exposed on their flanks, and finding a defence in an old Cyclopean wall, which can still be traced round the summit, the

Lacedaemonians were able to repel their assailants; and they were determined not to surrender. At length a Messenian captain came to the Athenian generals and said that he knew a path by which he thought he could take some light-armed troops round to the rear of the Spartans. The hill on its eastern side falls precipitously into the bay; but the fall is not direct. The summit slopes down into a hollow, about fifty yards wide, and then the hill rises again into the cliff which falls sheer into the water. But at the south end of the cliff there is a narrow gorge by which it is possible to climb up into the hollow. Embarking in a boat on the eastern side of the island, the Messenians reached the foot of the gorge and climbed up with difficulty, unseen by the Spartans, who neglected what seemed an impracticable part of the hill, and then ascending the summit suddenly appeared above the Lacedaemonians, who were ranged in a semicircle below on the western and northern slopes. The Athenians now invited the defenders to capitulate, and with the consent of their friends on the mainland they laid down their arms. Two hundred and ninetytwo, of the four hundred and twenty, survived, and were brought to Athens. The high opinion which the Greek world held of the Spartan spirit was expressed in the universal amazement which was caused by this surrender. Men had thought that nothing could induce the Lacedaemonians to give up their arms.

Cleon had performed his promise; he brought back the captives within twenty days. The success was of political rather than military importance. The Athenians could indeed ravage Lacedaemonian territory from Pylos, but it was a greater thing that they had in the prisoners a security against future invasions of Attica and a means of making an advantageous peace when they chose. It was the most important success gained in the war, and it was a brilliant example of the valuable successes that can be gained, as it were accidentally, in following that system of strategy which Pericles had laid down at the beginning of the war. This stroke of luck increased the influence of Cleon. It was necessary for Nicias to do something to maintain his reputation. Shortly afterwards he led an army into the Corinthian territory, gained a partial victory at Solygea, and then went on to the peninsula of Methone, between Troezen and Epidaurus. He built a wall across the isthmus and left a garrison in Methone. In the following year, he made the more important acquisition of the island of Cythera, from which he was able to make descents upon Laconia. The loss of Cythera was in itself more serious for Sparta than the loss of Pylos; but owing to the attendant circumstances the earlier event made far greater stir. The Athenians had now three bases of operation in the Peloponnesus—Pylos, Cythera, and Methone.

To none was the discomfit of the Spartans in Messenia sweeter than to the Messenian exiles who had borne their part in the work of that memorable day. At Olympia there is a figure of Victory, hovering aloft in the air, amid wind-blown drapery, while an eagle flies below her. It is the work of the sculptor Paeonius, and it was dedicated by the Messenians in the Altis of Zeus, with part of the spoil they stripped from the hated usurpers of their land.

Sect 11. Athenian Capture of Nisaea

In each of the first seven years of the war, Attica was invaded, except twice; on one occasion, the attack on Plataea had taken the place of the incursion into Attica, and, on another, the Peloponnesian army was hindered by earthquakes from advancing beyond the isthmus. Every year by way of reply the Athenians invaded the Megarid twice, in spring and in autumn. The capture of Pylos affected both these annual events. The invasion of Attica was discontinued, because Athens held the Spartan hostages; and the elation of the Athenians at their success induced them to undertake a bolder enterprise against Megara.

Minoa, now a hill on the mainland but then an island, lay at the entrance to the harbour of Nisaea. It was separated from Nisaea by a narrow channel, protected by two projecting towers. Nicias had destroyed these towers, three years before, and had fortified Minoa, so as to blockade completely the port of Nisaea. The Megarians then depended entirely on the port of Pagae and their communications with the Crisaean Gulf. They were hard pressed; their distress was vividly pourtrayed in the comedy of the *Acharnians* which was put on the stage two years later. The situation became almost intolerable when a domestic sedition led to the expulsion of a small party who seized Pagae and cut off Megara from importing food on that side too. It became a question between allowing the exiles to return or submitting to Athens. Those who knew that the return of their rivals from Pagae would mean their own doom opened secret negotiations with Athens, and offered to betray Megara and Nisaea. The Long Walls and Nisaea were held by a Peloponnesian garrison. The generals Hippocrates and Demosthenes organised the enterprise. While a force of 4000 hoplites and 600 horse marched overland by Eleusis, the generals sailed to Minoa. When night fell, they crossed to the mainland. There was a gate in the eastern wall close to the spot where it joined the fortification of Nisaea, and near the gate there was a hollow out of which earth to make bricks had been dug. Here Hippocrates and 600 hoplites concealed themselves, while Demosthenes, with some light-armed Plataeans and a band of the youthful Peripoloi or Patrollers of Attica, took up a position still nearer the gate, in a sacred enclosure of the war-god, Enyalios. The conspirators had long matured their plan for admitting the Athenians. As no boat could openly leave the harbour, owing to the occupation of Minoa, they had easily obtained permission of the commander of the Peloponnesian garrison to carry out through this gate a small boat on a cart at night, for the alleged purpose of privateering. They used to convey the boat to the sea along the ditch which surrounded Nisaea, and, after a midnight row, return before dawn, and re-enter the Long Walls by the same gate. This became a regular practice, so that they carried out the boat without exciting any suspicion, on the night fixed for executing the conspiracy. When the boat returned, the gate was opened, and Demosthenes, who had been watching for the moment, leapt forward and forced his way in, assisted by the Megarians. They kept the gate open till Hippocrates arrived with his hoplites, and, when these were inside, the Long Walls were easily secured, the garrison retreating into Nisaea. In the morning the main body of the Athenians arrived. A scheme for the betrayal of Megara had been concerted. The conspirators urged their fellow-citizens to sally forth and do battle with the Athenians; they had secretly arranged that the Athenians should rush in, and had anointed themselves with oil, as a mark by which they should be known and spared in the assault. But their political opponents, informed of the scheme, immediately rushed to the gates and declared decisively that they should not be opened; the battle would have to be first fought inside. The delay apprised the Athenians that their friends had been baffled, and they set about blockading Nisaea. Their energy was such that in two days the circumvallation was practically completed, and the garrison, in want of food (for their supplies were derived from Megara), capitulated. Thus the Long Walls, which they had built themselves, and the port of Nisaea had passed again into the hands of the Athenians. They were not, however, destined to take the city on the hill. The Spartan general Brasidas, who was recruiting in the north-east regions of the Peloponnesus for an expedition to Thrace, hastened to the relief of Megara. Nothing more than an indecisive skirmish took place; the Athenians did not care to risk a battle and they resolved to be content with the acquisition of Nisaea. Soon afterwards there was a revolution in Megara. The exiles from Pagae were received back; they soon got the power into their hands and njurdered their enemies. A narrow oligarchical constitution was established. The new order of things, says Thucydides, lasted a very long time, considering the small number of its authors.

Sect. 12. Athens fails in Boeotia

The recovery of Nisaea which had been lost by the Thirty Years' Peace was a solid success, and it seemed to the ambitious hopes of the two generals who had achieved it the first step in the recovery of all the former conquests of their city. Hippocrates and Demosthenes induced Athens to strive to win back what she had lost at Coronea. But Boeotia was not like Megara; and an attempt on Boeotia was an unwise reversion to the early continental policy of Pericles, which Pericles had himself definitely abandoned. The dream of a second Oenophyta was far less likely to come true than the threat of a second Coronea. And the enterprise was a departure from the Periclean strategy, of which Nicias was the chief exponent, and it is significant that Nicias took no part in it. Moreover at this moment Athens, as we shall see, ought to have concentrated her forces on the defence of her Thracian possessions which were in grave jeopardy. The Boeotian, like the Megarian, plan was formed in concert with native malcontents who wished to overthrow the oligarchies in the cities, to establish democratical governments, and probably dissolve the Boeotian Confederacy. At this time the Confederacy was governed by eleven Boeotarchs, two of whom were chosen by Thebes, and four Councils, of unknown nature and functions.

The new Boeotian plan, in which Demosthenes was now concerned, did not involve such extensive operations and combinations as that which he had conceived when he invaded Aetolia. But the two places resembled each other in so far as each involved operations from the Crisaean Gulf. Demosthenes, having sailed to Naupactus and gathered a force of Acarnanians, was to go on to secure Siphae, the port of Thespiae, on the shore of a promontory beneath Mount Helicon. On the same day, the Athenian army under Hippocrates was to enter Boeotia on the north-east and seize the temple of Apollo at Delium, which stood on the sea-coast over against the Lelantine plain in Euboea. At the same time Chaeronea, the extreme west town of the land, was to be seized by domestic conspirators. Thus on three sides the Boeotian government was to be threatened; and the same day was fixed for the three attacks. But the scheme was betrayed by a Phocian, and frustrated by the Boeotarchs, who occupied Siphae and Chaeronea with strong forces, and made a general levy of the Boeotians to oppose the army of Hippocrates. It mattered little that Demosthenes made a mistake about the day fixed for the attack; he found himself opposed by a Boeotian force and could only retire. None of the internal movements in the Boeotian cities, on which the Athenians had counted, took place.

Hippocrates, however, had time to reach and fortify Delium. He had a force of 7000 hoplites and over 20,000 light-armed troops. A trench, with a strong rampart and palisade, was drawn round the temple; and at noon on the fifth day from their departure from Athens the work was completed. The army then left Delium, to return home. When they crossed the frontier and entered the Athenian territory of Oropus, at about a mile from Delium, the hoplites halted, to wait for Hippocrates, who had remained behind to give final directions to the garrison of the temple; the light-armed troops proceeded on their way to Athens. The hoplites were interrupted in their rest by a message from Hippocrates, ordering them to form instantly in array of battle, as the enemy were upon them. The Boeotian forces had been concentrated at Tanagra, about five miles from Delium; and they had been persuaded by Pagondas, one of the Theban Boeotarchs, to follow and attack the Athenians in their retreat although they had left Boeotia. After a rapid march, Pagondas halted where a hill concealed him from the view of the Athenians and drew up his army. It consisted of 7000 hoplites—the same number as that of the enemy—1000 cavalry, and over 10,000 light-armed men. The Thebans occupied the right wing, in the unique formation of a mass twenty-five shields deep; the other contingents varied in depth. The Athenian line was formed with the uniform and regular depth of eight shields. Hippocrates had arrived and was moving along the lines encouraging his men, when the enemy, who had for some time been visible on the crest of the hill, raised the Paean and charged down. The extreme parts of the wings never met, for watercourses lay between them. But the rest pushed shield against shield and fought fiercely. On the right the Athenians were victorious, but on the left they could not sustain the enormous pressure of the massed Theban force, especially as the Thebans were probably man for man stronger than the Athenians through a laborious athletic training. But even the victory on the right was made of none effect through the sudden appearance of a squadron of cavalry, which Pagondas, seeing the situation, had sent unobserved round the hill. The Athenians thought it was the vanguard of another army and fled. Hippocrates was slain and the army completely dispersed.

The battle of Delium confirmed the verdict of Coronea.

The Boeotians were left masters of the field, but Delium itself was still held by the invader. This led to a curious negotiation. The Athenians demanded their dead, and the Boeotians refused permission to take them unless they evacuated the temple of Apollo. Now if there was an international custom which was universally recognised among the Greeks, even among the barbarous Aetolians, it was the obligation of the victor to allow his defeated opponents to remove and bury their dead, unconditionally. This custom had the sanction of religious feeling and was seldom violated. But in this case the Boeotians had a pretext for departing from the usual practice. They alleged that the Athenians had on their side violated the laws of Hellenic warfare by seizing and fortifying the sanctuary of Delium and living in it, as if it were unconsecrated,—using even the sacred water. There seems little doubt that the conduct of the Boeotians was a greater departure from recognised custom than the conduct of the Athenians. The herald of the Athenians made what seems a foolish reply, to the effect that Delium having been occupied by the Athenians was now part of Attic soil, and that they showed the customary respect for the temple, so far as was possible in the circumstances. "You cannot tell us to quit Boeotia," he said, "for the garrison of Delium is not in Boeotia." The Boeotians made an appropriate answer to the quibble: "If you are in Boeotia, take what is yours; if you are in your own land, do as you like." The dead were not surrendered, and the Boeotians betook themselves to the blockade of Delium. They took the place by a curious device. They sawed in two and hollowed out a great beam, which they joined together again very exactly, like a flute, and suspended a vessel by chains at the end of the beam; the iron mouth of a bellows directed downwards into the vessel was attached to the beam, of which a great part was itself overlaid with iron. This machine they brought up from a distance on carts to various points of the rampart where vine stems and wood had been most extensively used, and when it was quite near the wall they applied a large bellows to their own end of the beam and blew through it. The blast, prevented from escaping, passed into the vessel, which contained burning coals and sulphur and pitch; these made a huge flame and set fire to the rampart, so that no one could remain upon it. The garrison took flight and the fort was taken. The Boeotians no longer refused to surrender the dead, who included rather less than 1000 hoplites.

Sect. 13. The War in Thrace. Athens loses Amphipolis

The defeat of Delium eclipsed the prestige of Athens, but did not seriously impair her strength. Yet it was a fatal year; and a much greater blow, entailing a permanent loss, was dealt her in her Thracian dominion.

The war in Thrace was always complicated by the neighbourhood of the kingdoms of Thrace and Macedonia. Before the fall of Potidaea the Athenians had formed an alliance with Sitalces, king of Thrace, and made his son Sadocas an Athenian citizen. The realm of Sitalces extended from the Strymon to the Euxine, its coast-line began at Abdera and ended at the mouth of the Ister. His revenue of tribute both from Greek towns and barbarians amounted, in the reign of his successor, to more than 400 talents—counting only what was paid in the shape of coin. The alliance with Athens seems to have lasted till the king's death. An Athenian ambassador from Thrace, in the *Acharnians* of Aristophanes, reports to the Assembly:

> We passed our time
> In drinking with Sitalces. He's your friend,
> Your friend and lover, if ever there was one,
> And writes the name of Athens on his walls.

Perdiccas, the shifty king of Macedonia, played a double game between Athens and Sparta. At one time he helped the Chalcidians against Athens, at another he sided with Athens against her revolted allies. Throughout all changes of fortune, the city of Methone, situated to the south of the mouth of the Haliacmon, held to Athens with unshaken fidelity, though the varying relations between Athens and Perdiccas must have seriously affected the welfare of the Methonaeans. Some decrees relating to Methone have been preserved on a marble, adorned with a relief of the Athenian Demos seated, stretching out his hand to the Demos of Methone, who stands accompanied by a dog.

Perdiccas and the Chalcidians (of Olynthus) feared that the success of Pylos might be followed by increased activity of the Athenians in Thrace, and they sent an embassy to Sparta, requesting help, and expressing a wish that Brasidas might be the commander of whatever auxiliary force should be sent. It was wise policy for Sparta to threaten her rival in Thrace at this juncture, though the prospect of any abiding success was faint. No Spartans went, but 700 Helots were armed as hoplites; the government was glad to take the opportunity of removing another portion of this dangerous element in the population. Having obtained some Peloponnesian recruits and having incidentally, as we have already seen, saved Megara, Brasidas marched northward to the new colony of Heraclea.

Brasidas was a Spartan by mistake. He had nothing in common with his fellows, except personal bravery, which was the least of his virtues. He had a restless energy and spirit of enterprise, which received small encouragement from the slow and hesitating authorities of his country. He had an oratorical ability which distinguished him above the Lacedaemonians, who were notoriously unready of speech. He was free from political prejudices, and always showed himself tolerant, just, and moderate in dealing with political questions. Besides this, he was simple and straightforward; men knew that they could trust his word implicitly. But the quality which most effectually contributed to his brilliant career and perhaps most strikingly belied his Spartan origin was his power of winning popularity abroad and making himself personally liked by strangers. In Greece, the Spartan abroad was a proverb for insolence and misbehaviour. Brasidas shone out, on a dark background, by his frank and winning manners.

His own tact and rapid movements, as well as the influence of Perdiccas, enabled Brasidas to march through Thessaly, which was by no means well disposed to the Lacedaemonians. When he reached Macedonia, Perdiccas required his assistance against Arrhabaeus, the king of the Lyncestians, in Upper Macedonia. Brasidas was impatient to reach Chalcidice, and he contrived to make a separate arrangement with Arrhabaeus and abstained from invading Lyncestis, to the disappointment of Perdiccas. He then marched against Acanthus, situated on the base of the peninsula of Acte. The mass of the Acanthians were perfectly content with the position of their city as a member of the Athenian Confederacy; they had no grievance against Athens; and they were unwilling to receive the overtures of Brasidas. They were, however, induced by a small party to admit Brasidas alone into the city, and give him a hearing in the Assembly. From his lips the Acanthians learned the Lacedaemonian programme, and Thucydides has given the substance of what he said. "We declared at the beginning of the war that we were taking up arms to protect the liberties of Hellas against Athens; and for this purpose we are here now. You have a high repute for power and wisdom, and therefore a refusal from you will retard the good cause. Every city which joins me will retain her autonomy; the Lacedaemonians have pledged themselves to me on this point by solemn oaths. And I have not come to be the tool of a faction, or to enslave the many to the few; in that case we should be committing an act worse than the oppression of the Athenians. If you refuse and say that I have no right to thrust an alliance on a people against its will, I will ravage your land and force you to consent. And for two reasons I am justified in doing so. The tribute you pay to Athens' is a direct and material injury to Sparta, for it contributes to strengthen her foe; and secondly, your example may prevent others from embracing freedom." When Brasidas retired, there was a long debate; much was said on both sides. The manner of Brasidas had produced a favourable impression; and the fear of losing the vintage was a powerful motive with many for acceding to his demand. The vote was taken secretly and the majority determined to detach themselves from Athens, though they had no practical grievance and were not enthusiastic for the change.

Acanthus was an Andrian colony, and its action led to the adhesion of two other Andrian colonies, Stagira and Argilus; and the relations which Brasidas established with Argilus led to the capture of the most important of all Athenian posts in Thrace, and among the most important in the whole Athenian empire, the city of Amphipolis. This place, of which the foundation has been already recorded, had diminished the importance of Argilus and roused the jealousy of the Argilians; although some of the colonists were of Argilian origin. The coming of Brasidas offered Argilus an opportunity, for which she had been waiting, against the Athenians of Amphipolis. After a cold wintry night march, Brasidas found the Bridge of the Strymon defended only by a small guard, which he easily overpowered. Amphipolis was completely unprepared, but Brasidas did not venture to attack the city at once; he expected the gates to be opened by conspirators within, and meanwhile he made himself master of the territory.

That a place of such first-rate importance as Amphipolis should be found unprepared at a time when an energetic enemy like Brasidas was actively engaged against other Athenian cities in the neighbourhood seemed a criminal negligence on the part of the two Strategoi to whom defence of the Thracian interests of Athens was entrusted. These were Thucydides, the son of Olorus, and Eucles. It was Negligence inexcusable in Eucles, who was in Amphipolis, to leave the Bridge without an adequate garrison; and it was considered culpable of Thucydides to have removed the Athenian squadron to the island of Thasos, where (it was insinuated) he possessed mines of his own. A message was sent at once to Thucydides; that officer hastened back with seven triremes and reached the mouth of the Strymon in the evening of the same day. But in the meantime Brasidas had offered the inhabitants of Amphipolis such easy terms that they were accepted. He promised every citizen who chose to remain equal political rights, without any loss of property; while all who preferred to go were allowed five days to remove their possessions. Had the Amphipolitans known how near Thucydides was, they would probably have declined to surrender. Thucydides arrived just too late. But he preserved Eion, at the mouth of the river, and repelled an attack of Brasidas.

The true blame for the loss of Amphipolis probably rests not on the General, who was in a very difficult position, but on the Athenians, who, instead of making adequate provision for the defence of Thrace, were misled by the new strategy of Demosthenes into the unsuccessful expedition to Boeotia. It must be remembered that Thucydides was responsible for the safety of the whole coast of Chalcidice and Thrace; that at any moment he might be summoned to defend any part of it from Potidaea to the Chersonese; that therefore either Eion or Thasos was a suitable centre for his headquarters; and that Eion had the disadvantage of having no harbour.

It may be that we are indebted to the fall of Amphipolis for the great history of the war. The Athenians accused the neglect of their generals, as having cost them one of their most valuable possessions. Thucydides was sentenced to banishment, and it is probable that Cleon, to whom he bore no good-will, was instrumental in drawing down upon him a punishment which possibly was not deserved. But in his exile the discredited general became the greatest of Greek historians. If he had remained at Athens and completed his official career he might never have discovered where his genius really lay. By travelling in foreign lands, among the enemies of Athens and in neutral states, Thucydides gained a large knowledge of the Hellenic world and wrote from a wider point of view than he could have done if he had only had an Athenian experience. "Associating," he says himself, "with both sides, with the Peloponnesians quite as much as with the Athenians, because of my exile, I was thus enabled to watch quietly the course of events." Judged in this way, the fall of Amphipolis, a great loss to Athens, was a great gain to the world.

Having secured the Strymon, Brasidas retraced his steps and subdued the small towns on the high eastern tongue of Chalcidice. The

Andrian Sane and another place held out, and their obscurity saved them. Brasidas hastened on to gain possession of Torone, the strongest city of Sithonia. A small party of the citizens invited and expected him; but the rest of the inhabitants and the Athenian garrison knew nothing of his coming until the place was in his hands. Torone was a hill city by the sea. Besides its walls, it had the protection of a fort on a height which rose out of the water and was connected with the city by a narrow neck of land. This fortress, known as Lecythus, was occupied by an Athenian garrison. Brasidas halted within about half a mile from the city before daybreak. Seven bold soldiers, light-armed and carrying daggers, were secretly introduced by the conspirators. They killed the sentinels on the top of the hill, and then broke down a postern gate, and undid the bars of the great gate near the market-place, in order that the men without might rush in from two sides. A hundred targeteers who had drawn near to the walls dashed in first, and when a signal was given Brasidas followed with the rest. The surprise was complete. Fifty Athenian hoplites were sleeping in the agora; a few were cut down; most escaped to the fort of Lecythus, which was held for some days and then captured.

Brasidas called an assembly of the Toronaeans, and spoke to them in words which sounded strange indeed falling from the mouth of an Hellenic victor. He told them that he had not come to injure the city or the citizens; that those who had not aided in the conspiracy to admit him would be treated on a perfect equality with the others; that the Lacedaemonians had never suffered any wrong from Torone; and that he did not think the worse of those who opposed him.

Sect. 14. Negotiations for Peace

In the meantime the Athenians had taken no measures to check the victorious winter-campaign of Brasidas. Their inactivity was due to two causes. The disaster of Delium had disheartened them, and rendered the citizens unwilling to undertake fresh toil in Thrace. In Grecian history we must steadfastly keep in view that we are reading about citizen soldiers, not about professional soldiers; and that the temper of the time, whether of confidence or dismay, modifies all the calculations of military and political prudence. Secondly, the peace party, especially represented by the generals Nicias and Laches, took advantage of this depression to work in the direction of peace. The possession of the Spartan captives gave the means of coming to terms with Sparta at any moment, but it was clear that they could not now conclude a peace on such favourable terms as would have been possible a year before. If an able statesman, like Pericles, had at this time possessed the confidence and guided the counsels of the Athenians, he would have persuaded them to postpone all thought of peace until the success of Brasidas had been decisively checked and the prestige of Athens in some degree retrieved. This was obviously the true policy, which would have enabled Athens to win the full advantage of the captives of Sphacteria. It was a policy which Cleon, a far abler politician than any of his opponents, must have preached loudly in the Assembly. But the Athenians were not in a mood to weigh considerations of policy; they were swayed by the feelings of the hour, which were flattered by the arguments of the military experts; and they decisively inclined to peace.

The Lacedaemonians were more deliberately set on peace than the Athenians. Their anxiety to recover the Sphacterian captives peace. increased, and on the other hand they desired to set a term to the career of Brasidas in Chalcidice. They wished to take advantage of the considerable successes he had already won, to extort favourable conditions from Athens before any defeat should undo or reverse his triumphs. Nor was the news of his exploits received at Sparta with unmixed feelings of pleasure. They were rather regarded with jealousy and distrust. The victories had not been won by an army of Spartan citizens, but by the brilliant un-Spartan qualities of Brasidas and a force of which the effectiveness entirely depended on its leader. Brasidas had broken through the fetters of Lacedaemonian method, and his fellow-citizens felt that he was a man of different fibre from themselves, and suspected and disliked him accordingly. Moreover the personal influence of king Pleistoanax was thrown weightily into the scale of peace. This king had been banished just before the Thirty Years' Peace, on the ground that he had taken bribes to spare Attica when he invaded it after the deliverance of Megara. He had lived for nearly twenty years in western Arcadia on the mountain of Lycaeon, beside the dread sanctuary of Zeus, of which it was told that whosoever entered it lost his shadow and died before the year was out. Even here Pleistoanax was afraid for his life. His house was half within the precincts, so that in case of danger he could retire into the sacred place without passing his door. But he had influence at Delphi, and whenever the Spartans consulted that oracle they were always bidden to take back into their own land the seed of the demi-god, the son of Zeus, or else they would have to plough with a silver share. The Lacedaemonians at length recalled him, and re-enthroned him as king with ancient and most solemn ceremonies. But his enemies now vexed him with the charge of having bribed the Pythian priestess to procure his recall. Pleistoanax conceived that such charges would fall to the ground if he satisfied the people by negotiating a permanent peace and restoring as speedily as possible the prisoners from their captivity in Athens to their impatient friends at home. And as a matter of fact, Sparta had everything to gain from making peace at once, unless she was prepared to adopt the Imperial policy of Athens, against which it had been hitherto her role to protest. Such a policy might for a time have met with some success if she had put her whole confidence in Brasidas, but must soon have been checked by the naval superiority of her rival.

Pleistoanax and Nicias understood each other; and Nicias, a man of commonplace ability and possessed by one idea, played into the hands of Sparta. It was not, however, an easy matter to arrange the exact terms of a durable pacification, while it was important for Athens that the negotiation should be made before she experienced any further losses in Thrace. Accordingly the two states agreed on a truce for a year, which would give them time to arrange quietly and at leisure the conditions of a permanent peace. The truce and some of its conditions were suggested by Athens; the terms were drawn up at Sparta and accepted by the Spartan Assembly; and were then conveyed to Athens, where they were proposed for the acceptance of the Athenian Assembly by Laches. The clauses were the following: (1) Free access to the Delphic oracle was ensured to all. For Athens had been debarred from consulting it during the war. (2) Both parties guaranteed the protection of the treasures of Delphi. (3) During the truce both parties should keep what they had; the Athenians retaining Pylos, Cythera, Argolic Methone, Nisaea, and Minoa. (4) The Lacedaemonians were not to sail, even along their own coasts, in warships or in merchant vessels exceeding a certain size (twelve tons). (5) The free passage of envoys, for the purpose of arranging a peace, was provided for. (6) Neither party was to receive deserters; and (7) disputes, in case they arose, were to be decided by arbitration.

The truce was sworn to. But in the meantime an event happened in Chalcidice which was to disappoint the pacific calculations of the statesmen at Athens and Sparta. The city of Scione on the western prong of the Chalcidian fork revolted from Athens and invited Brasidas, much to that general's surprise. For it was far more hazardous for the towns on the peninsula of Pallene to defy the authority of Athens than for any others; since by the strong city of Potidaea, which stretched entirely across the narrow isthmus, they were isolated and as much exposed to the full force of Athenian power as if they had been islanders. The arrival of Brasidas and the words he spoke to them wound up the men of Scione to the highest pitch of enthusiasm; they set a golden crown on his head, as the liberator of Hellas, and their admiration for him personally was shown by casting garlands on him, as if he were a victorious athlete,—so great was his popularity.

At this point an Athenian and a Lacedaemonian commissioner arrived to announce the truce, which had in fact been concluded two days before Scione revolted. The Athenians refused to admit Scione to the benefit of the armistice until the authorities at home had been consulted. There was deep indignation at Athens when the news of the defection of Scione arrived; it was practically the rebellion of "islanders" relying on the land-power of Sparta. Cleon was able to take advantage of this exasperation and carry a decree that Scione should be destroyed and all the male inhabitants slain. This incident brings out in an interesting way the geographical difference between the three sea-girt promontories of Chalcidice as to their degrees of participation in the insular character. Acte, with its steep inhospitable shores, is far more continental than insular; Sithonia partakes of both natures more equally, is more strictly a half-island; Pallene is more an island than part of the mainland. And we see the political importance of such geographical differences. The loss of Scione produces an irritation at Athens which the loss of Torone could not inspire.

The revolt of Scione was followed by that of the neighbouring town of Mende, and although this happened distinctly after the truce had been made, Brasidas did not hesitate to accept the alliance of Mende, his plea being that in certain points the Athenians themselves had broken the truce. The case of Mende differed from that of Scione; for the revolt was the doing not of the people but of an oligarchical faction. Brasidas was then obliged to join Perdiccas in another expedition against Arrhabaeus, king of the Lyncestians. The fact that the Macedonian monarch was contributing to the pay of the Peloponnesian army rendered it necessary for Brasidas to co-operate in an enterprise which was of no interest to the Greeks. Arrhabaeus was defeated in a battle, but a reinforcement of Illyrians came to his help, and the warlike reputation of Illyria was so great that their approach produced a panic among the Macedonians and the whole army of Perdiccas fled, leaving the small force of Brasidas to retreat as best it could. He was in great jeopardy, but effected his retreat successfully. The incident led to a breach between Brasidas and the Macedonians; Perdiccas changed sides once more, and proved his new friendship to Athens by preventing Lacedaemonian troops, which had been sent to join Brasidas, from crossing Thessaly.

Brasidas returned to Torone and found that an Athenian armament of fifty ships, under Nicias and Niceratus, had recovered Mende, and was besieging Scione. Everywhere else the truce was observed, and by tacit consent the hostilities in Thrace were not allowed to affect the rest of Greece. But it was inevitable that they should frustrate the purpose for which the truce had been concluded. It was impossible that negotiations with a view to the definitive peace should proceed in exactly the same way as had been originally contemplated; by the end of the year there was a marked change in public feeling at Athens and the influence of Cleon was again in the ascendant. If Nicias had played into the hands of Sparta, Brasidas had played into the hands of Cleon and effectually embarrassed the home government. His conduct first in regard to Scione and then in regard to Mende was unjustifiable and entirely governed by personal considerations. The gold crown of Scione seems to have acted like a potent spell in arousing his ambition, and he began to play a war-game of his own. His policy was the more unhappy, as he was perfectly aware that it was impossible to protect the cities of Pallene against the fleets of their indignant mistress. He effectually hindered the conclusion of peace, which his city sincerely desired. Brasidas and Cleon, Thucydides says, were the chief opponents of the peace; but while the motives of Brasidas were purely personal, the policy of Cleon, whatever his motives may have been, was statesmanlike. He adopted the principle of Pericles that Athens must maintain her empire unimpaired, and he saw that this could not be done without energetic opposition to the progress of Brasidas in Thrace. The charge of Thucydides that Cleon desired war because he could not so easily conceal his own dishonesty in peace, does not carry the least conviction. When the truce expired, Cleon was able to carry a resolution that an expedition should be made to reconquer Amphipolis. It does not appear whether he was himself anxious for the command, in consequence of his previous success at Pylos, or whether the opposition and lukewarmness of the strategi practically forced him into it. But it is certain that all possible difficulties were thrown in his way by Nicias and the peace party, who in their hearts doubtless hoped for the complete failure of his enterprise.

Sect. 15. Battle of Amphipolis and Peace of Nicias

Cleon set sail with thirty ships, bearing 1 200 Athenian hoplites, 300 Athenian cavalry, as well as allies. Taking some troops from the force which was still blockading Scione, he gained a considerable success at the outset by taking Torone and capturing the Lacedaemonian governor; Brasidas arrived too late to relieve it. Cleon went on to the mouth of the Strymon and made Eion his headquarters, intending to wait there until he had augmented his army by reinforcements from Thrace and Macedonia.

Not far from its mouth the stream of the Strymon expands into the lake Kerkinitis; on narrowing again into its proper channel it is forced to bend to the westward in order to skirt a hill, and forms a great loop, before it disgorges its waters into the sea close to the walls of Eion. In this loop the high city of Amphipolis stood, water-girt as its name implies,—the river serving as its natural defence, so that it required artificial bulwarks only on the eastern side. On the right bank of the river, to the west of the town, rose the hill of Cerdylion; on the east were the heights of Pangaeus. A ridge joined Pangaeus with the hill of Amphipolis, and the wall of the city crossed the ridge. The Strymon Bridge was outside the southwestern extremity of the wall; but, since the place had passed into the hands of Brasidas, a palisade had been built connecting the bridge with the wall. Brasidas with some of his forces took up a commanding position on the hill of Cerdylion, from which he had a wide view of the surrounding country; while other troops remained in Amphipolis under the command of Clearidas, whom he had appointed governor. Their hoplites numbered about 2000.

The discontent and murmurs of his troops forced Cleon to move prematurely. The soldiers had grumbled at leaving Athens under an utterly inexperienced commander to face a general like Brasidas, and they were now displeased at his inaction. In order to do something, Cleon led his army to the top of the ridge, near the city wall, where he could obtain a view of the country beyond, and, as he saw Brasidas on Cerdylion, he had no fear of being attacked. But Brasidas was resolved to attack, before reinforcements should arrive; and, seeing the Athenians move, he descended from Cerdylion and entered Amphipolis. The Athenians, who had reached the ridge, could observe the whole army gathered within the city, and Brasidas himself offering sacrifice at the temple of Athena; and Cleon was presently informed that the feet of men and horses, ready to sally forth, could be seen under one of the gates. Having verified this fact for himself, Cleon gave the signal to wheel to the left and retreat to Eion; it was the only possible line of retreat, and necessarily exposed the unshielded side to an enemy issuing from the city. But he made the fatal mistake of not preparing his men for action, in case they should be forced to fight; he rashly calculated that he would have time to get away. Hence when Brasidas, with 1 50 hoplites, came forth from one of the gates, ran up the road, and charged the Athenian centre, the left wing, which was in advance, was struck with terror and took to flight. At the same time the rest of the garrison of Amphipolis, led by Clearidas, had issued from a more northerly gate and attacked the Athenian right. Here a stand was made, though Cleon, unused to the dangers of warfare, proved himself no better than many of his hoplites, who were said to be the flower of the army. He fled, and was shot down by a targeteer. But the bravery of Brasidas was doomed as well as the cowardice of Cleon by the equal decree of Death. As he was turning to assist Clearidas, he received a mortal wound and was carried into the city. He lived long enough to be assured of the utter rout of the foe; but his death had practically converted the victory into a defeat. The people of Amphipolis gave him the honours of a hero; they made him their founder, and removed all the memorials of the true founder of their colony, the Athenian Hagnon. Sacrifices were offered to Brasidas, and yearly games celebrated in his honour.

The death of Brasidas removed the chief obstacle to peace; for no man was competent or disposed to resume his large designs in Thrace. The defeat and death of Cleon gave a free hand to Nicias and the peace party. The peace party were in truth far more responsible for the disaster than Cleon, whom they had placed in a false position. Thus the battle of Amphipolis led immediately to the conclusion of peace; and the comic poet could rejoice in the destruction of the pestle and mortar—Cleon and Brasidas—with which the spirits of War and Tumult had pounded the cities of Greece. But the desire of peace seems to have been even stronger at Sparta than at Athens, where there was a certain feeling, in spite of the longing for a rest from warfare, that the lustre of the city was tarnished and something strenuous should be done. Menaces of invading Attica were required to apply the necessary pressure; though they could hardly have been seriously contemplated, as long as the captives were in an Athenian prison. Negotiations were protracted during autumn and winter, and the peace was definitely concluded about the end of March.

The Peace, of which Nicias and Pleistoanax were the chief authors, was fixed for a term of fifty years. Athens undertook to restore all the posts which she had occupied during the war against the Peloponnesians: Pylos, Cythera, Methone, Atalanta, and Pteleon in Thessaly. But she insisted upon retaining Sollion and Anactorion, and the port of Nisaea. The Lacedaemonians engaged to restore Amphipolis, and to relinquish Argilus, Stagirus, Acanthus, Scolus, Olynthus, Spartolus, which cities, remaining independent, were to pay a tribute to Athens according to the assessment of Aristides. Moreover, the fortress of Panacton, in Mount Cithaeron, which the Boeotians had recently occupied, was to be restored to Athens. Certain towns in the possession of Athens, such as Torone, were to be dealt with at the discretion of Athens. All captives on both sides were to be liberated.

It appeared immediately that the situation was not favourable to a durable peace; for, when the terms were considered at Sparta by a meeting of deputies of the Peloponnesian allies, they were emphatically denounced as unjust by three important states, Corinth, Boeotia, and Megara. Corinth was indignant at the surrender of Sollion and Anactorion; Megara was furious that Nisaea should be abandoned to the enemy; and Boeotia was unwilling to hand over Panacton. Yet

Athens could hardly have demanded less. The consequence was that the Peace was only partial; those allies which were politically of most consequence refused to accept it, and they were joined by Elis; the diplomacy of Nicias was a complete failure, so far as it aimed at compassing an abiding peace. But since the deepest cause of the war lay in the commercial competition between Athens and Corinth, and since the interests of Sparta were not at stake, the treaty might seem at least to have the merit of simplifying the situation.

But, if we admit the justification of the imperial policy of Pericles, then the policy of vigorous action advocated by Cleon was abundantly justified. It may safely be said that if the conduct of the state had rested entirely with Cleon, and if the military talents of the city had been loyally placed at his disposal, the interests of Athens (as Pericles understood them) would have been far better served than if Nicias and his party had been allowed to manage all things as they willed without the restraint of Cleon's opposition. Few statesmen of the merit of Cleon have come before posterity for judgment at such a great disadvantage, condemned by Thucydides, held up to eternal ridicule by Aristophanes. But when we allow for the personal grudge of Thucydides, these testimonies only show that Cleon was a coarse, noisy, ill-bred, audacious man, offensive to noblemen and formidable to officials—the watchful dog of the people. Nothing is proved against his political insight or his political honesty. The portrait of Aristophanes in the *Knights* carries no more historical value than nowadays a caricature in a comic paper. He too had suffered from the assaults of Cleon, who

> had dragged him to the Senate House,
> And trodden him down and bellowed over him,
> And mauled him till he scarce escaped alive.

The Peace, The Peace of Nicias was celebrated by a play of Aristophanes which admirably expresses the exuberant joy then felt at Athens, but carefully avoids the suggestion of any noble sentiment that may have quickened the poet's delight in the accomplishment of the policy he had advocated. So Cleon's friends might have said; but we must judge Aristophanes fairly, and not misapprehend the comic poet's function. Comedy did not guide public opinion, but rather echoed it; comedy set up no exalted ideal or high standard of action. The best hits were those which tickled the man in the market-place and more or less responded to his thoughts. Aristophanes had his own political prejudices and predilections; but as a son of Athens he was assuredly proud of the great place which her democracy had won for her in the world. It was the nature and the business of his muse to distort in the mirror of comedy the form and feature of the age; but the poet who was inspired to write the verse

O rich and renowned, and with violets crowned, O Athens, the envied of nations!

cannot have been altogether out of sympathy with those who strove to maintain the imperial position of his country.

Made in the USA
Coppell, TX
11 February 2020